D0930000

Am I Still AUTISTIC?

How a Low-Functioning, Slightly Retarded Toddler
Became the CEO of a Multi-Million Dollar Corporation

John Hall

Am I Still Autistic?

Copyright © 2011 by Opportunities In Education, LLC.

All rights reserved. No part of this publication may be
reproduced, distributed, or transmitted in any form
or by any means, including photocopying, recording,
or other electronic or mechanical methods,
without the prior written permission of the publisher,
except in the case of brief quotations embodied in critical
reviews and certain other noncommercial uses permitted
by copyright law. For permission requests, write to the
publisher, addressed "Attention: Permissions Coordinator,"
at the address below.

First Printing, 2011

ISBN 978-0-615-49523-1

Opportunities In Education, LLC.,
1507 7th Street, Suite 460, Santa Monica, California 90401,
info@amistillautistic.com.

www.amistillautistic.com

Graphic Design by
Stephanie Starr (steffstarr@aol.com)

Printed in U.S.A

In Loving Memory Of My Parents,
Katherine & John Robert Hall Jr.

And Dedicated To My Son,
John Robert Hall IV (J.R.)

Table of Contents

1
Where I Came From

Imagine you are in the kind of calm, tranquil, altered-consciousness state people aspire to when they meditate. Imagine you feel no tension or stress whatsoever, neither in mind, body, or spirit. Your entire psyche is enveloped in peace and comfort. Nothing bothers you.

Outside noises are meaningless. Time is meaningless. You move through life with complete serenity, utterly unperturbed by whatever beings and sounds exist around you.

Here is the good news: if your son or daughter is autistic, that is where they live, in that beautiful, peaceful, totally comfortable world. Nothing bothers them; nothing causes them pain or disrupts their contentment—until you or someone else intrudes on their private space.

My son lives there. Even when he is pushed or pulled out of his altered state of consciousness, he avoids connecting with me, my wife, his sister, and everyone else. Unless someone interacts with him, is in his face every moment, he retreats into his private world where he is perfectly happy, completely safe, and thoroughly comfortable.

I know exactly how he feels.

I used to live there, too.

My memories of being autistic are quite lucid. I did not cognitively realize I was different, of course, but I clearly remember having that sense of peace and contentment. Incessantly messing with pots and pans or flushing the toilet was comforting. I felt like a happy, healthy, normal child.

If you asked me today, "How would you like to flip a light switch on and off for the next three hours?" I would consider it the most monotonous torture anyone could imagine. But then? It was soothing. I would do it until someone physically moved me from the switch, away from being able to reconnect with the switch. It is what I did. You could yell at me for five minutes-right in my face, even right in my ear-and I would not respond. Yes, I would hear what you said, but your words, your tone, your expectation of a reaction were meaningless to me. Nothing penetrated the shield protecting my private world. I lived in an entirely different albeit visible dimension. All babies initially exist in their own worlds, of course, but mine, like my son's, never expanded. I remained closeted in my personal space: content, peaceful, comfortable. The ultimate Alpha high.

Today I can easily recognize the differences between normal children and the kind of toddler I was. All I have to do is watch my own son and daughter. I now understand, for example, that most children have inherently short attention spans. My daughter gets bored playing with the same toy after just a little while and comes to her mom, dad, or grandmother looking for her next amusement.

I possessed no sense of time passage whatsoever. And I never went to my mother looking for anything. Ever.

My daughter notices when my wife is happy or angry with her. Lia can sense when it is a good time to ask for something and when it is time to stop being stubborn and simply obey. If she wants attention, she runs to someone for a hug, tugs on a pant leg, or pouts, cries and makes demands. Standard kid stuff.

My son never knows when anyone else is happy or upset. The concept of other people's emotions does not exist in his world. He hears me speak to him but does not respond. I know just what he is feeling when that happens: nothing. He is only barely, peripherally aware that another person is in front of him unless I reach out and pull him to me. He can watch the water swirl down a shower drain for twenty minutes in a state of perfect bliss while I sit by, feeling helpless and depressed. He does not get bored, he does not call for me to, "Look, look, Daddy! Look!" At age four, when other boys whoop through the house leaving untold destruction in their wake, he plays with his trains for long periods of time, lining them up in the repetitive-ritualistic manner known as "stimming."

While my daughter comes over to say, "Hi Daddy!" and just hang out with me, my son stands in front of the television and watches whatever is on the screen until someone turns it off or moves him away.

My daughter will ask, beg, plead, cry, or throw a tantrum to get her way. My son, passive and compliant, will communicate basic needs ("Juice. Milk.") but is otherwise disconnected from getting his way. He has no "way." Totally withdrawn from engagement, he does not crave being held or sung to or even noticed.

Those things simply do not exist in his world, just as they did not exist in mine.

I can only suspect how my mother felt when I was diagnosed as severely autistic, but I certainly know I did not want to hear those words applied to my son, and avoided accepting them as long as I could. Luckily, we already knew he was academically gifted; my initial diagnosis included slight retardation. And, unlike my son, my prognosis was not good. I was low functioning. The best my parents could expect for me was decades of therapy, which could possibly—but not necessarily—lead to a menial job in the distant future. I would need special assistance my entire life. The "American Dream" of my going to regular school, making friends, attending college, and having a family of my own was not in the cards for me.

Sometimes even experts are remarkably wrong.

There are no physical tests for autism, no exact diagnoses and no sure-fire cures. Every child is different, and no two births, environments or developmental circumstances can possibly be identical. Nevertheless, those early intervention experts who so confidently predicted my bleak future rocked back on their heels with astonishment at how much my mother and I flipped that prognosis on its ear. Yes, it took decades of hard work and skin thickening, but from the moment my mother thrust me into the real world unprotected by therapists and protocols, my life veered off their forecasted road for good. In very little time I discovered I actually liked people and wanted friends—and for someone as fiercely determined to remain disconnected in his own private world as I was, that alone was a complete 180-degree reversal.

Learning how to first get along, and then become friends with other people was arduous to say the least; at times, it was almost unbearably onerous. Over the course of years, I acted out, acted obnoxious, and acted confident when I was scared to death. For my misguided efforts I was bullied, ostracized, and beaten up. But I listened and watched and experimented and tried until, eventually, I became so alert to other people's emotional, mental, and social cues that noticing and responding to them has now become almost second nature.

Was it worth all the struggle and sorrow, the back-sliding and plunging forward, the emotional push-push-push?

I write these words as a thirty-five-year-old, fully integrated adult who has earned a bachelor's degree, a Master's degree, and is now sitting for his doctorate. I easily make friends and retain healthy relationships. I am CEO of a thirteen-year-old national company that I helped found and which continues to grow, thanks in no small part to my social skills and outgoing personality.

Do I still have to focus to successfully manage some interactions that other people take for granted? Yes. Am I still working through lingering issues stemming from my autistic childhood? Sure-but none I cannot overcome. And that encompasses both the salient point and the primary motivation for this book. Succinctly put: the impossible is possible. Autism can be overcome. If I can do it, my child can, too.

And so can yours.

2
I Was Happy, They Weren't

I always felt normal. As far back as my earliest memories, I felt like a happy, healthy, normal child. I felt comfortable-especially comfortable. When I turned the light switch on and off, on and off, on and off until my mother wanted to scream, I felt peaceful and content. I was not bored. I was not confused. I was not even oblivious to the world around me. I knew people were there; I heard their voices. I did not respond to those voices partly because I did not know how and partly because responding was not comfortable, not part of my "normal." Pulling all the pans out of the cabinets and bang-bang-banging them, flushing the toilet over and over again, and controlling the light switch repeatedly, endlessly, exasperatingly for my parents, was.

My mother and father, of course, did not agree with my unspoken concept of "normal." In November, 1976, when I was a year-and-a-half old, my mom took me to a mother/toddler group in the Preschool and Infant Parenting Service at Cedars-Sinai Medical Center. The Child Development Specialists there did not agree with my view of "normal," either. They took my not responding to people as being "mute." They viewed my usual occupations as "ritualistic behavior" that "tuned out" the environment. They contended that I "rejected people as a source of gratification and security" and "relied on myself for tension reduction." They were probably right.

I was born John R. Hall, III on March 5, 1975 to Katherine and John R. Hall, Jr. My dad was fifty-five years old, a gentle soul who believed in God, in contrast to my much younger Jewish mother, who did not. Dad was a successful, loving but passive, almost docile man, genteel as a result of his Southern heritage and upbringing. He had already lived a full life by the time he met my mother. He had left his childhood home in Alabama to fight in World War II, relocated to California to become a successful salesman, and enjoyed a long, albeit childless, marriage to a woman who eventually died from a brain aneurism. During her hospitalization, he met my mother, two and a half decades his junior. He essentially went from one marriage to the next.

Mom was precisely everything Dad was not: strong, passionate, and aggressively independent. Raised in Southern California by Eastern European immigrants, she had left home at sixteen to earn an architectural degree and make her own way in the world. Her father, who was roughly the same age as mine and had joined the Marines to also fight in World War II, was probably the genetic donor of her all-encompassing intensity. In fact, he once told her she had more balls than any of her three younger brothers.

Except for rare occasions when obligation or need took a hand, Mom had little use for Dad's family or her own. Her sense of independence had morphed into a need for isolation by the time I was born: she also eschewed religion and the general concept of making or having friends. Holding positions typically reserved in those days for men, she was accomplished and determined and viewed motherhood as her most important project-one for which she paid an abnormally high price.

My birth was not smooth. I was born with fluid in my lungs at a new hospital that did not have the equipment or facilities to handle that kind of neonatal emergency. I was immediately taken from my mother and sent across town by ambulance to what was then Cedars of Lebanon Hospital. By the time we got there, my lungs had cleared up, but the doctors nevertheless kept me in the neonatal unit for a day or two, when they pronounced me healthy enough to go home.

Unfortunately, my mother was not so lucky; my birth had almost killed her. Years later, the doctors would determine she had a severe case of Lupus. Then, they only knew that she was extremely ill, dangling between life and death. She remained hospitalized for two or three weeks and was still pretty sick even after she came home. She was not able to become directly involved in my care for two or three months.

My dad was very active for his age, but I was his first child, and he thought he was too old to be a parent. He had no idea what to do with, about, or for me. My parents had arranged for a nurse to take care of me, a very formal, old-school British nurse, who must have been in her sixties and who I can now only imagine: even though she stayed with us for a year, I have no cognizant memory of her. Nevertheless, I doubt I bonded with her or any of the hospital nurses. I obviously had no chance to bond with my mother because of her illness; I do not think she was even able to hold my hand during those first few weeks. I apparently did not bond with my father due to his reticence. And as an inadvertent result of my mother's tendency toward isolationism, I also clearly did not bond with anyone in either of my parents' families.

Looking back, I suspect that initial isolation, which

my infant psyche undoubtedly took as abandonment, probably contributed to my autistic behavior. Experts I have spoken to recently agree. In the mid-1970s, however, that simply was not the thought process. Even though everyone who became involved in my care and rehabilitation knew what had happened to me, no one gave it serious credence.

And yet, how much effect could it have had? My son, John R. Hall IV, was showered with love and affection from the moment he emerged from the womb. My wife was ill before and after childbirth, but I opted to stay with J.R. throughout that first tenuous day and never let go of his tiny hand. Leilani's nature is significantly gentler than my mother's was, and unlike my father, I have taken an active role in my son's care since the day he was born. Nevertheless, J.R. lives in the same detached, secluded world I did.

In his famous 1950s "Monkey Love Experiments," University of Wisconsin psychologist Harry Harlow showed:

... mother love was emotional rather than physiological, substantiating the adoption-friendly theory that continuity of care—"nurture"—was a far more determining factor in healthy psychological development than "nature." Second, he showed that capacity for attachment was closely associated with critical periods in early life, after which it was difficult or impossible to compensate for the loss of initial emotional security.

The biggest differences between my son's autism and mine center on our natures and early academic abilities. Was I more aggressive because of my early seclusion? Was my mental development delayed because no one cuddled me? Is my wife's sweet soul the reason our son does not act out or sit crying for hours, unable to control his anger and frustration? I do not know; I do not think anyone ever will.

By the time my mom was healthy enough to take

care of me herself, I must have been a rude awakening for her. I did not respond the way a normal baby responds to his mommy. I did not reach for her or cry when she left. I did not play "peek-a-boo," and her logs indicate this bothered her a lot. I did not look for her to hold me. When she held out her arms, I did not run into them for a hug. I was already installed in my private, separate world, and while I might play next to her, I would not necessarily play with her. Going down the developmental guidelines that I have since come to know so well with my own children, I did not "resist the unfamiliar." I did not demand attention or "test for curiosity." I would not imitate-another aspect that upset my mom quite a bit. And I did not communicate. By the stage that other kids formed words, I only babbled, and I did not point or try to communicate with gestures. I never invited responses or obeyed because those things did not exist in the altered-consciousness state, where opening and closing doors, flushing toilets, flipping light switches, and banging pots and pans consumed and delighted me. I did not cry when my mother removed me from a repetitive activity; I simply moved on to another one. In clinical parlance, I "showed no attachment behavior."

Neither, apparently, did my mother.

Whether because she had experienced such a blow health-wise or because my behavior so bewildered her, my mother initially expected as little of me as I offered. If I projected any clues about what I wanted or needed, she did not pick up on them, an incongruity noted in the initial Cedars-Sinai Preschool and Infant Parenting Service report written after she had taken me in to be evaluated by Dr. O. Ivar Lovaas, one of the world's leading autism experts. That state did not last long, however. By the time we began the Cedars-Sinai Home Intervention Program under Shelley Gallenson's twice-weekly observation, my mother's response to my lack of response was jumbling through concern, irritation, and a fierce determination to connect with her only son.

"Fierce" and "intense" were keywords to describe my mother's life. I suspect they unintentionally contributed to my discomfort and reinforced my desire to remain sequestered in my Alpha state. My comfort level was to be just with myself, a disposition my mother took as both a matter of concern and, incongruously, a deliberate affront to her. The more troubled she became about my withdrawal, the more intense her own behavior grew; the more intense her behavior, the more I withdrew. Between us, we established a vicious cycle of miscommunication, anxiety, determination, and love that would define our relationship until the day she died.

She may have gotten off the parenting mark a little late, but my mom would not be deterred. She intensely followed the dictates of the program to set aside specific short bursts of time when she would play with me in specific ways with specific toys or games. According to the logs she kept with an architect's meticulously detailed care, I responded pretty quickly to her efforts with a desire to please her, be with her, and capture more of her attention. Unfortunately, I did not have the tools or understanding of how to ask for that attention in an appropriate way outside of those times when Mom tuned into me, so I "acted out."

I bit, hit, scratched, pinched, screamed, kicked, and threw things to get notice, smiling all the while. That smile—which my wife and I understand to mean our son is trying to communicate in a positive way—acted like a proverbial red flag to my mother. The therapists may have thought I was mildly retarded, but my mother's intuition told her I was so bright that even as a toddler, I had the cognitive ability to premeditate my tantrums. "He does little things that he knows are naughty with a smile as a test." My behavior was always personal to her, as if, for some reason, I was being abnormal just to spite her.

My mother and I maintained this dynamic throughout most of my childhood. Looking back, I have to believe she did not actually understand what was going on with me or why I did what I did. For my part, I know I had no idea about how to read my mother's—or anyone else's—cues for good behavior. Once I started wanting attention, I did whatever I could to get it. It might have been my own form of fierceness or intensity, but the smile on my face during my attention-getting tantrums was meant to indicate that I had good intentions. I simply did not know any other way to behave. If my development was, in fact, arrested, it was not for lack of effort on my part. Simply put, I wanted Mommy, I wanted her now, I wanted her for my own and I wanted her to stay. At ages two and three, I exhibited the needs of a just-awakened newborn.

My mother did not have the time or temperament for that level of neediness, however, and never accepted the near-retardation or low-functioning-autistic diagnoses as an explanation. Instead, she truly believed everything I did, good or bad, was calculated and purposeful. A case in point: I had a significant bond with my great aunt, who I called Nana. She was very soft and sweet with me, extremely compliant, and would pretty much do whatever I wanted her to do: pick me up and carry me, play with me, get me a cookie. My mother was so certain my behavior was deliberate that once when I was barely two years old and Nana visited, Mom noted in her therapy log, "... he really played us against each other."

As an adult dealing with my own son's slow development, I understand my mom's frustration. I can even appreciate why she thought I was intentionally manipulating her. She was strong, a fighter, but here she was being reduced to tears by a little child who not only threw tantrums, which was bad enough, but who, from her perspective, willfully withheld affection. How could I possibly not know what I was doing?

I had never seen him so hateful and distant. Now that tantrums have subsided, it's easier, but the reduction of affection and that spiteful biting is hard on our egos. I am so tired that each irritation is amplified. Why won't he talk or at least mimic? He also won't play "Where's Mommy's eyes?" though he'll point out Pooh Bear's eyes. Well...the end of the tantrums should be enough of a breakthrough, I guess.

As hard as it was for her to accept, I was absolutely and completely unaware of my effect on her or anyone else. I never meant to be nasty to anyone, never wanted to get under anyone's skin, never had the capacity to devise the contest-of-wills my mother projected onto my conduct. I wanted to feel comfortable. When I withdrew into flipping that light switch, I was comfortable—-even though the more I did it, the more intense my mom became about making me stop. She would call my name over and over, but—unlike my perfectly healthy daughter, who will hear me calling but ignore me—I heard my mother but did not ignore her. I simply had no response. I had no reflex. I existed in a separate world. Her words were meaningless to me, her commands equally hollow. We were wholly unconnected.

When the Cedar's-directed home program pried me out of my shell enough that I began wanting to connect, I might as well have been set adrift on the ocean when it came to how to connect, despite my mother's absolute conviction that I could if I wanted to. When I felt threatened or beleaguered, I instinctively withdrew into my safe, contented world and returned to my comforting rituals.

Transitioning immutably into my mother's "real" world was slow, cumbersome, jolting, fraught with backslides, and often maddening for all concerned. Contrasting my behavior with J.R.'s once again, however, I cannot help but notice the disparity between me being

22

my mother's most important project, and J.R. being my wife's most important son.

3
Cracking My Shell

In February, 1977, one month before my second birth-day, Mother and I began going to Cedars-Sinai a few times a week so Shelley Gallenson, our Home Intervention child-development specialist, could "work" with me more closely. My mom was not driving at the time, so we traveled by bus from our condo in Santa Monica to the clinic in West Hollywood. It took three buses to get us there and three more to get us home, but Mom was committed to my getting whatever therapy I needed.

I was no longer mute, as I had been during my initial evaluation four months earlier, but according to the entries in my mother's logs, written in the blockish, almost-calligraphic hand of the professional architect, I still "refused" to make the sounds she wanted me to make, such as "buh" for bottle. I also apparently got "very nervous and cranky" around people other than my parents. During a visit to my grandparent's house with my Alabaman

25

Uncle Jim and Cousin Bud, for example, my mother recorded: "Played but insisted on John or I there (in sight) constantly. At dinner table, John and I both had to be there. When we got home again, just John, J.R. and I, was fine and playful."

My mother's logs are fascinating: they spell out everything she felt, everything she observed, and everything Shelley recommended. Looking at them now from the distance of several decades, I can clearly correlate my mother's frustration with my lack of developmental progress and my increasingly aggressive behavior—both of which I know were linked to my growing awareness and desire to connect to her coupled with my persistent inability to figure out how. We were trapped in a mutually aggravating quagmire. She had taken herself in hand and made herself into a strong, formidable, independent individual; she fully expected me to have inherited the ability to do the same. And perhaps I had—looking back over my life, I undoubtedly did—but I was too young, too frightened, and too bewildered to understand anything beyond, "I want Mommy. I see Mommy—Mommy see me? I want Mommy."

As far as Shelley and the Cedars-Sinai Department of Psychiatry was concerned, my persistent inability to connect was the result of "severe developmental delay" and could be overcome, or at least somewhat improved, via a series of techniques that had helped many children. Unfortunately, those standard psycho-educational techniques did not take our unusual dynamics into consideration. She drove me to be driven; I realize now what a blessing that turned out to be, but no one can deny that it made both our lives difficult in the interim. Though neither of us realized it at the time, my biting, screaming, throwing, nose-picking/booger flinging, and other inappropriately aggressive behaviors actually constituted the rawest form of an escalating fortitude that ultimately ensured my success, even while creating ever more obstacles to reaching that success.

Was all that ferocity necessary? Did I have to mimic my mother's intensity via the most off-putting behaviors available? I cannot answer that, but I can say that although I love my son dearly and feel very, very blessed to have him, I was initially as restrained with him as my mom was with me. She was reticent because she did not know how to help me. I held back because, although I do know how to help him, I also know exactly what he is going through now and what he will have to deal with to be successful once he finally and fully emerges from his private world. I went through the motions but could not relate to him. I was too frightened for him-and for myself.

Then Lia came along, our "normal" child who connects as naturally as she breathes. She opened me to an entire world of possibility and potential and made me realize I did not have to be afraid about my son. It will take time, but J.R. and I will connect. I am as dedicated to this as my mother was to connecting with me. But I have made the decision to not become too intense about it. I truly believe he can make it without having to scratch and claw through every step along the way.

My mother did not have a second child to bring her to this awareness. She may have thought our relationship was harder on her than on me—"Withholding bottle is difficult—more so on me than him. I'm so tired. The crying and whining are agony"—but I distinctly remember those crying sessions. I would get so frustrated and bewildered and agitated I simply could not stop myself or even catch my breath. And yet, reading between the lines, I see now that I was, in fact, connecting with my mom: I was unintentionally mimicking her disposition.

Consider that family gathering with Uncle Jim and Cousin Bud. Mom noted, "I wanted so much for him to be good when John's relatives were here and when I finally got out." Clearly, she was apprehensive and anxious about what might happen and frustrated about what her life had become, feelings I manifested with my own nervous, cranky behavior, just as my happy, playful attitude mirrored her relief when we got home. I may not have met her eyes or understood how to act the way she wanted me to, but I definitely responded to the intensity of her feelings.

"Intensity" radiates from Mom's logs. I was under almost constant assessment while in the intensive psycho-educational program at the clinic, where I essentially played one-on-one with a therapist within a group of similar children and received individual psychotherapy three times a week. I eventually graduated to the High-Risk Mother/Toddler program in the Cheerful Helpers Preschool and then the Therapeutic Nursery School program. As the surrounding adults coaxed me from the safety of my private world, I incorporated the most prominent aspect of my mother's nature into mine: her intensity. I did not know how to relate; I did not even understand the connect-the-dots of life beyond "do this, get cookie." But the more my mother and therapists drew me out of my shell, the more insistent, anxious, and needy I became-not exactly the result they were looking for-and the more avidly I wanted attention and connection. The more insatiable my needs became, the more aggressive, anxious, confused, and frustrated my mother's log entries became.

He wants to swallow me up all day. If I am busy, there's whining. Any activity I try (phone calls, reading the paper, needlepoint), gets constant bothering, some positive attention getting, some negative (whining, biting me, grabbing out of my hands). I am very angry all of [a] sudden. His big 45-minute tantrum Thursday seemed to touch me off, and it gets progressively worse. My every move is governed by his needs, sometimes his wants, and I have to buy peace. In return, he is just not putting out. When I see reversion, no matter how

28

"normal" it is, I am furious. Furthermore, every step forward is costing me a psychological fortune. We are closer, we relate, but he won't say a word! What was coming out is fewer and farther between.

The therapy is costly. I feel some pressure to fix everything quickly, and no matter how I try, it seems like it may be forever. John says, "When's it all going to end?" Logic tells me that he is coming along, but he fights me on every front. One minute he thrills me with some new antic, and then makes me struggle days for the next bright star. Meanwhile, I feel that the toehold dwindles and weakens.

When I first read my mom's journals as a young adult, I felt bad about these kinds of entries. When I think about it from my current perspective as a father, I clearly see the connection between Mom's need to "fix everything quickly," Dad's longing to know "when's it all going to end," and my increasingly aggressive need to figure out some way to get the attention I craved, be it positive or negative. The need for connection between Mom and me was so strong and powerful, it was palpable, forceful.

Aggressive.

I might never have understood what caused my transformation from peacefully content to raucously aggressive if I had not examined the juxtaposition of my mom's logs and my wife's relationship with my son. My mother was uncompromisingly fixated on my getting better and staying that way. She would do anything possible to help me succeed at her quest and honestly could not comprehend why I did not respond in quid pro quo. She fought me on every front as much as I fought her. It was a remarkable connection, yet one she did not see and certainly would not have condoned or accepted if she had.

And so we fought on, both side-by-side and face-to-face, neither understanding what we were doing to the other, neither understanding how to get what we wanted from the other, yet both intensely dedicated to achieving the same result: connection to the other.

4
Weapons of Resistance

My battles with Mom were never played out on a level field. I bit her. I hit her, scratched her, pinched her, and obsessed over her feet. I never looked her in the eye-instead, I looked at her hands, her cheek or almost anywhere else. I gestured and made babbling, incomprehensible sounds but did not speak or answer questions. Sometimes I screamed for no reason or made a noise so upsetting it made her "blood run cold," and she would "rush to interact" with me.

I did not drink anything out of a cup except water, and I did not sit still to eat. In fact, I often did not eat at all, and when I did, often spat out the food. I frequently returned to flipping light switches, pulling out pots and pans, flushing toilets, and other repetitive behaviors my mother had labeled "no-nos." The only things she could parry with were disciplinary guidelines that she felt were age-appropriate and the grit of her will against mine. It was a completely lopsided contest: her reason and ex-

31

pectations against my barely peripheral awareness that she did not want me to do certain things-an awareness that did not reach the level of making me understand or care. Can I have Mommy now?

My smiling while committing "no-nos" added a nerve-rattling element to our battles and accentuated how disconnected we were. My mother dismissed the psychotherapeutic theory that I smiled to show I was trying to connect positively, but my memories support that notion-when people smiled at me, it made me happy. I liked feeling happy, so I smiled at them, even if they were not smiling at that precise moment, even if I was doing something my mother did not like me to do.

"I guess he doesn't take in what you're saying," Shelley explained to my mom at one point. She was right: I did not take in my mom's passionate directives to stop whatever she told me to stop, nor her equally passionate words of help and encouragement. I eventually developed to the point that my teachers considered me gifted, but back while I was still withdrawing, I simply did not understand what Mom's words meant. I have no idea why it took me so long to get there-perhaps those particular synaptic pathways simply had not yet begun to fire. Whatever the reason, Mom just could not wrap her brain around the idea that my lack of understanding was organic, not malicious.

Mom was absolutely certain-utterly convinced beyond discussion-that I turned to "purposeful bad, destructive, dangerous behavior, laughing at discipline" whenever possible. All my "misbehavior" and "negative relating" was the result of spite or meanness—no other explanation made any sense to her, no matter how many times "Shelley says ....", entries rationalized it differently. According to Mom, I wore either a "nervous little smile" or a "taunting and chiding grin." When I was compliant and interested in what she was doing in the kitchen, for example, I was a wonderful little boy, but

32

when I lost her attention for whatever reason and tried to get it back using whatever methods I knew, I became a monster with whom, at one point, she was afraid to be alone.

Even if I had not been a special-needs child, I doubt I could have figured out how to "taunt" or "chide" at such a young age. I think about my own daughter—yes, she can be defiant, but I cannot see her having that kind of cognitive or strategic reasoning. Nevertheless, my mother, who had no patience for her own frailties, certainly was not going to give credence to mine. It was an odd twist of logic: she readily admitted not only that I needed assistance but also that she needed help of her own to provide that assistance. However, she was not about to accept that I did not somehow possess superior intent of purpose and a remarkable, apparently inborn malice.

That was Mom: she went through life accentuating the negative and minimizing the positive. She was a loud, forceful, in-your-face, passionate woman who undertook projects and brought them to successful, even stunning completion with brisk, if sometimes brusque efficiency. For the first twenty years or so of my life, I honestly thought the woman could do no wrong. She pushed and pulled and demanded; she forced me to "accomplish" whether or not I thought I could, was ready, or had any foundation for what I was doing. We had plenty of disagreements about everything—especially what I was or was not doing with my life—but I always assumed that everyone recognized and respected her as a miracle problem-solver, an extraordinary individual who could work out almost any challenge, crisis, or problem. And I was her biggest challenge, her most important project. She was absolutely determined to solve me. But for all her ardent love and capabilities, she could not sanction the audacious concept that my behavior was an intricate part of my developmental problems. She knew, without question, that I could understand, I could control,

I could comply if I would just apply myself. When I did not, it simply had to be because I "patently refused" to do so. This was incontrovertible fact to her. And so we battled on, her with her unconditional lines in the sand, me with my smiling lack of comprehension.

According to her logs, though, I was not the only one intentionally attacking her. I don't know if she was like this before I came along or if the combined challenge of me and her own physical decline caused a little "poor me" paranoia, but those writings are full of pressures she felt from just about everyone with whom she regularly engaged on my behalf. She took suggestions, observations, and even casual comments as assaults on her diligence, her intelligence, or her compliance. As chief assailant, I struck on a much more personal level, of course: I attacked her patience, her resolve, and her love. According to my mother, I used a stockpile of weapons to either exert control or "get" her and my dad—sometimes deemed a positive effort, sometimes deemed a negative—but often without any provocation.

First and foremost, of course, was my anger. She saw all my biting and throwing and pinching and hitting as either a display of "unprovoked" anger or my attempt to punish her with "spiteful" anger. She was so invested in this idea that she once admitted she feared my anger meant I did not love her.

I did love her. I loved her more than I could ever articulate, and I wanted so very much to please her. She was intense, crisis-driven, and constantly stressed, so I became intense, crisis-driven, and stressed. From the distance of three decades, it makes perfect sense. I naturally existed in a beautiful world of peace and comfort. Whenever someone aborted my soothing repetitive action or forced me to recognize and interact with them, I felt jolted and disoriented. The Cedars-Sinai people probably understood the trauma of this shift from the soothing Alpha state to a beta awakening; their program

34

therapists and home-based therapeutic companions always approached me softly and gently, as did my dad and other relatives. But Mom was looking for results, and time was running out! When she pulled my hand from whatever "no-no" I was doing, got in my face about playing with the toys she wanted me to learn, or prodded me to speak more clearly, my knee-jerk physical reactions flawlessly mirrored the vigor of her "urgency." In the long run, taking on her fierce determination would become my saving grace, turning into a constant internal drive that pushed me to do better, get stronger, learn more, and engage further. As a three-year-old, though, with "speech organs [that] have had limited use," my unconscious mimicry of her compulsive nature obviously felt like a frontal attack to her, thereby feeding her anger, which incited my anger, which made her feel besieged....

She did eventually concede to at least some part in this cycle of miscommunication. "My relaxed and at-peace mode is complimenting his as well as reinforcing it, in the same way my frustration, anger, and fatigue bring his negative emotions to the surface." Later, she noted, "I do not want him to sense any urgency on my part as that has always worked against what we are trying to do, even when I tried to hide that urgency." Those entries of recognition are easily overlooked-buried as they are amidst pages and pages of details about my nasty, negative behavior—but they are there. On some level, she knew we were in this together. In one telling item, she dutifully notes:

Shelley suggests: It is again possible that he cannot control his negative behavior or that he thinks he cannot stop it himself. It is also possible that he is not cognizant of the fact that his negative behavior causes us to discipline him. He may be taking in only the discipline and experiencing us as mean and angry, which in turn makes him angry.

My mother may have written these words, but later entries make it clear she did not actually believe them. She decided, for example, that the "anxiety noise" that made her blood run cold was yet another device I intentionally employed because when she "rushed to interact" with me, I was "not always anxious ... sometimes just bored or playing alone." Later she wrote, "Reversion to anxiety noise but in different context. Not when bored or anxious-to rather mock communication with pointing and gestures." Even for Mom, that was an amazing motivation to assign to a small child.

Another apparent weapon in my arsenal of deliberate misbehavior was language, or my lack thereof, about which my mother was zealous. She notated every sound I uttered and every association she imagined I made with each sound. I was not alone in this particular face-off; the nursery school teachers and therapeutic companions were all in on it, not encouraging me enough to verbalize rather than gesture, not consistently demanding I speak more clearly. Mom's logs are full of notations about Shelley telling her, "(once again) to hold back on power struggles over speech," but my mother knew that language was a key to the normal life she envisioned for me. "When asked, [he] often mouths words without sound (he wants to say it but doesn't want us to know)." She was absolutely overjoyed when, after she had begun working outside the house on a regular basis, I began speaking more often and more clearly.

Language: incredible, appropriate, spontaneous-no hesitation, no delay-language in public places, among strangers, spontaneous and upon request, with obvious pleasure. It is like a whole new world for us all—his discovery that he can get us or what he wants in a new positive way! Every day is an exciting adventure for us as well, watching his new recognition and comprehension of his world and his delight with it. Every word knocks us over. Even his chattering yields two syllable

sounds-seeds of words that we can watch germinate.
Fathom this...I can no longer list his full vocabulary.

Possibly the most confounding weapon in my quiver was my quest for attention. I apparently never let her or my dad have any space to breathe. If left alone, I would immediately slip into my private world and engage in one of those "no-no" behaviors I was supposed to leave behind, so Mom could not let me simply be-but she also could not fathom why, having been told so many times, I "patently refused" to stop doing the things that shaped my comfort, or why, when jolted from that peaceful world, I would not quietly play by myself rather than strain for her attention.

This is another twist of logic I have to chalk up to Mom's powerful belief that whenever my behavior was "positive" it was because she had taught me to do it, and whenever my behavior was "negative" it was due to my purposely defying her. Playing quietly by myself meant flipping light switches, flushing toilets, or doing those other soothing, repetitive actions that allowed me to withdraw. Not doing those "no-nos" meant I had been coaxed or dragged into a fully awake state of mind where I incessantly craved interaction.

For me, life was an either-or situation: private world, interactive world. If Mom was tired, though, or did not feel well, or wanted to be on the phone or just have a conversation with my dad, she took my efforts to gain her attention as brutally intrusive and told me to play quietly by myself-which she then stopped me from doing because it meant slipping back into my repetitive-action space. She never understood the mutual-exclusivity of my two worlds, and I was much too young and confused to be anything but frustrated by demands that left me with no place to go. I "acted out" my confusion/frustration with "negative" behavior, of course, which Mom, having long forgotten or discarded Shelly's gentle prodding about my state of perception, regarded as deliberate and angry attacks.

I cannot find any semblance of recognition in her logs or even in our adult discussions that my still-underdeveloped brain did not function the same way her educated adult brain did. Her take on our cycle of miscommunication was: "He and I get caught up in the throes of negativism—he does it, I get angry, he is angry at my anger and does it again."

Regardless of my behavior, my mother only held off on returning to full-time employment until I was safely out of diapers. Not too surprisingly, our relationship improved radically as soon as she began leaving the house every day. My language skills continued to improved, my ability to let her and Dad have time together got better and easier, and even my behavior in the Cedars' nursery school improved.

As soon as [John] started the effort [to control that part of his life that is his to control], I relaxed, and J.R. sensed what was happening and resumed play alone and a general return to normalcy. Somehow, just sensing that this was a case of family dynamics, was enough to help me look at the situation objectively. The best part was how quickly J.R. snapped back when the climate improved.

That seemed to be the key: As much as Mom and I loved each other, we both seemed to be a lot happier and healthier when we did not spend too much time together. Thank you, Cedars-Sinai!

5
Between Shell and School

I remember my very first Cedars program. It was held
in a playroom with a large mirror I later discovered
was a one-way window in the parents' observation
room. Our playroom had a red, brown, and orange cir-
cular rug and a lot of toys. Shelley, who I already knew,
would get on the floor to interact with me for forty-five
minutes of play "therapy." She held up a toy, for example, and said, "What's this?" Or she asked me to say
my name, my dad's name, or her name. I now watch
my son's therapists use this same technique and have
learned to do it with him myself. Shelley always offered
an incentive for whatever "task" she wanted me to do: a
piece of candy, a puzzle, the chance to play with a favorite toy, or maybe just quiet time reading a book with
someone. My mom used this same technique at home,
but what felt scary and like a chore with her was fun at
school. Even though I spent most of my mornings with

someone always in my face, forcing me to interact, it never felt as intimidating as it did with my mother.

Once our individual therapy sessions were over, the teachers read to us and taught us basic things such as colors and shapes, all wrapped around therapeutic tasks. After nap time, we played. I'd ride around on a shiny tricycle or climb and run around in their huge blue structure. Then lunch, a visit to the park with one of my therapeutic companions, and then home. This was my "academic" experience from preschool through kindergarten; the only difference between the two programs was the classrooms. The "therapy" pretty much stayed the same. The kids pretty much stayed the same. We only had about seven or eight kids in my Cedars' classes—Neil, Beth, David, a bunch of others—but we always had a party every time someone's birthday came around. We learned a little more academically each year, but I was still way behind where my son is now at age four. The therapists were not trying to prepare us to enter mainstream society. They were merely trying to get us to stop biting and hitting, withdrawing into our individual private worlds, and avoiding eye contact. I, at least, was never expected to graduate from elementary school, much less high school. These things were not even a remote possibility for me as far as my teachers and therapists were concerned.

I was in good company. As the years went by, I was not the only one who continued biting and hitting now and then. Our teachers always stopped us, but I doubt any of us understood why we acted that way or why we should stop. I know I did not understand how to connect the dots between what I wanted and the best way to get it; I did not even know those dots existed. My behavior was pure impulse with only one goal: affectionate attention. If I could not figure out how to get affection, I certainly knew how to get attention.

I remember one such incident with my Uncle Cary,

Mom's youngest brother and a UCLA student at the time. Because Mom and Dad had to leave for work, he came over to the house every morning, made me waffles, and drove me to school. He let me sit up front in the passenger seat, and I really liked that.

On this particular day, we had gotten off the freeway and were stopped at a traffic light. Just as the car started moving again, I threw open my passenger-side door. I have no idea know why I did it, but I am pretty sure I had a smile on my face. Cary had to reach across me to slam it shut. Then he yelled.

I suppose a "normal" kid would have felt terrible for doing something bad or frightened by his uncle's anger. Actually, a "normal" kid probably would not have opened the door in the first place. But all I felt was sad. I always felt sad when I upset people; it was the only emotional association I could make at that point. I did not play with the door again, but not because I realized I had done something wrong or dangerous. I simply did not want to feel sad again about upsetting my uncle. Cause-and-effect, action-and-consequence were not part of my operating system.

Neither was making friends. Friends had never really been a priority for me, partly because my parents and I lived in a 317-unit New York style luxury apartment complex with a doorman, a gym, and a pool. This was before the state barred "No Children" discrimination, so kids were not allowed to live there, but as the complex's architect, my mom got a variance for me. However, that meant I had no other kids in the building to play with, and I was not encouraged to make friends with any of the kids I saw at the park. That was fine with my mother; she never had any of her own friends over—if she had any, which I doubt she did outside of work associates. She did not believe in wasting time with friendships. None of Dad's friends ever came over either. We lived a rather cloistered existence in our upscale, adults-only

Santa Monica condominium. My teachers and therapists may not have expected much for or from me, but my mom expected me to fit in, be a "little man," and conform to behavior suitable for our living conditions and her professional status. She loved me deeply and intensely, and she was not about to accept the notion that I could not behave properly if I wanted to.

I got to be very close friends with Neil and David and loved going for after-school play dates. Neil lived in Los Angeles and David in Culver City, so going home with them exposed me to far much more diversity than I could ever get at Cedars or at home. With my mother's attitude about friendships, I felt very special whenever Neil or David was allowed to come play at my house.

Those play times were always after school, never on a weekend. My parents and I had a special, private set of Saturday and Sunday rituals. Dad and I got up every Saturday morning, made chocolate pudding—I licked the bowl—then ate it together while watching *Bugs Bunny*. Dad never asked me to complete any tasks or act like "a little man." It felt wonderful to just be a kid with him and not have to live up to my mom's expectations for a few hours.

Of course, as soon as Mom came home from having her nails or hair done, she yelled at us about the mess we had made. Every week. Mom was very strict: everything had to be clean, everything had to be in its place, everything had to be structured. She always calmed down once the kitchen was cleaned up, after which the three of us went out to brunch before we did the week's grocery shopping.

When I was just with my dad, we ate at McDonalds. Apparently, we went there a lot when I was very young, probably because it was the only semi-safe place they could take me. I always found it relaxing and comfortable, although sometimes I almost felt as if I was doing something wrong when Dad and I went there alone. But when the family had lunch together on Saturdays, we usually went to an adult type of place where I had to eat some adult type of food and act as prim and proper as possible. Mom expected me to behave like a miniature adult, a chore for me at best, if for no other reason than my lack of eye contact. I did not get comfortable making eye contact with most people until years—actually, decades—later.

Looking at someone straight on and meeting their eyes was too intimate, too scary. The few times I tried it, I felt exposed and helpless, so I neither did it nor thought about it. As with so many other autistic traits, the people around me had more problems with my lack of ocular contact than I did. When something felt uncomfortable, I simply did not go there. Problem solved! But not for my parents and therapists. One of my therapeutic play "tasks" was always something like, "If you look at me here (pointing to their eyes), I'll give you a piece of candy." So I'd look at them and get the candy. They had myriad variations, but the idea was always the same: "Do you want this toy, J.R.?" they asked, holding it up next to their eyes. "Look at me and tell me and you can have it." I would look at them and babble whatever word they wanted to get the toy. The equation in my head was "answer question = get toy." That was all it meant to me. It was supposed to encourage the habit of looking in a person's eyes, but it did not.

When I started first grade, I still did not grasp that eye contact was a good thing that would help me make friends or connect with other people. I felt connected to my mom, dad, Nana, and Shelley, the four safest people in the world. What more did I need? For her part, my mother did not care about my making friends and connections; she cared that I did react appropriately when we were out in public and, more importantly, that I did not look directly at her. As a father, I understand her frustration perfectly. As a six-year-old, I had no idea what she was talking about.

On the other hand, I did have fleeting, sporadic eye contact with my dad when we hung out together on Sundays. We lived across from Palisades Park, about two miles north of the famous Santa Monica Pier. Every Sunday, we walked down through the park to ride the carousel and bumper cars on the pier. For lunch, I ate a grilled-cheese sandwich at a little restaurant that catered to the fishermen who docked their boats on the lower level. Sundays were fantastic. Dad was carefree, fun, and expected nothing more from me than to just be a kid. It was perfect.

Mom never went with us on Sundays. She did not like being outside, being in the sun, going swimming, or even getting her feet wet in the ocean. I imagine her still-undiagnosed Lupus had something to do with all that. Dad and I, on the other hand, loved the water and used the complex's pool together. Mom never came, not even just to watch. Nor was she the type to walk with us to the pier. My therapeutic companions took me to the park all the time, but I cannot remember ever seeing Mom there. Her approach to life—my life at least—was rather sterile, extremely intense. And almost entirely task-oriented. She was determined to make me well. As I experience my own son's progress, I have to agree with the experts that parents are not necessarily the right people to handle their children's therapy, and my mom is a perfect example of why. She never let a minute go by without assigning me a task or pushing me toward my full potential. On the other hand, if she had not demanded so much of me, would I be where I am now? I just do not know.

I know it would have been nice to have fun with her once in awhile. She never did things with me the way Dad did. A big USC football fan, he took me to their games at the Coliseum many times. I had no idea what was going on down on the field, but I loved the food. As soon as I finished my hot dog and chocolate malt, I was ready to go home! Dad took me to Disneyland, too, and did all the other things parents normally do with their kids. But it was always just me and Dad, which, looking back, was not necessarily bad. Mom would never have let me have a chocolate malt.

No, my time with Mom was structured, adult-like, and tense. Compared to my dad, she sometimes felt more like a caretaker than a loving mother, and I often thought she was just mean. Once in awhile, though, she turned into a really sweet, warm mommy. When she cuddled me on her lap, I got such a warm feeling in my heart that it brought chills to my body. Most times, her hugs and lap times felt forced, but on those rare occasions when she softened and was "Mommy," she was wonderful-like at my Kindergarten graduation.

We had a little ceremony in a multipurpose room. All the classes and all the parents were there, so it felt like a big deal. I was excited and sad at the same time. We all knew we were leaving for good. This was the last time we would be together! My mom was not comfortable with blubbering, but the therapists encouraged us to cry and I did. So did Mom. It felt wonderful.

The teachers made yearbooks for each of us, really cool blue photo albums with shiny covers filled with pictures of my family, the teachers who worked with me, and the kids in my program. Each photo had a little caption about who everyone was and what I liked to do. I loved looking at that book, even years later when Mom had to get it out of the special place she kept it in along with my baby book.

Shelley and my community of Cedars therapists and teachers, being "in the profession," as my mom once labeled them, were certain that I should move on to a special-education first grade. I needed to continue in small classes and slowly work my way up the developmental chain. They still considered me significantly delayed and pointed to my continuing language problems and aggressive behavior. Sending me to regular school, where I would be faced with twenty-five or thirty other students in a classroom that had only one teacher would put me at a tremendous disadvantage and essentially set me up for academic, emotional, and psychological disaster.

My mother vehemently disagreed. She knew—as she always had—that I could do more than they expected. She expected—no, she knew—I would be successful in regular school if given the opportunity to try. Over all protests, written and verbal, she arranged for me to start school, on time, in a regular classroom with a standard first-grade curriculum.

With that one decision, my mother totally altered the trajectory of my life away from perpetually disadvantaged and toward limitless possibilities.

God bless you, Mom.

6
First Grade

I had no business being in a mainstream first-grade class. I was miles behind academically, light-years behind socially. Most of my peers had been to regular preschool and kindergarten. They did not have to figure out how to talk or connect. They did not have to process what some kid meant when he sneered at them or what the teacher wanted them to do. They had social instincts, fundamental people skills, and an age-appropriate grasp of right and wrong.

On my very first morning at Roosevelt Elementary School, I told a girl I had just come from flying an airplane. I was serious-absolutely convinced I had flown that plane. I was so nervous, I just blurted it out.

I had good reason to be nervous. Ms. Savage's first-grade class was a huge change for me. I had never even been to the school before; many of the other kids had been there for kindergarten. Instead of a rug and shelves of toys, my new classroom had desks and thirty kids—

47

more kids than I'd ever seen at one time in my entire life. I wanted to impress them and make friends with them, but I was different from them in just about every way possible.

I looked different. Mom had dressed me, as usual, in a nice pair of pants and a tucked-in polo shirt. None of the other kids wore polo shirts. Most wore T-shirts or regular buttoned shirts and jeans. They all seemed so much more relaxed and acclimated than me.

They were ahead of me academically, too. I had learned my numbers, ABCs, and a few rudimentary words in kindergarten, but the other kids were beyond mere word recognition. Most could already read and do simple addition. They were also more used to advanced concepts. Every morning, we sat down as a group and listened to our teacher read to us from a chapter book, too long to be read in a single class. It took Ms. Savage two weeks to get through *James and the Giant Peach*. No one had ever read a big story like that to me. I was used to short books like *Good Night Moon* or *Runaway Bunny*. I loved it, but could not always remember what had been read the day before. No one else seemed to have that problem.

My ability to learn was not on par with the rest of the class, either. After story time, the aides came in and we broke into groups to work on our reading. I was in the "red thin reader" group. Most of the kids got through that fundamental book pretty quickly and moved on, but not me. The discrepancy between me and the other students quickly became painful. I had trouble sounding out the words, and then more trouble retaining those groupings in my head. I still did everything by rote the way I had learned at Cedars—say word, get cookie—but it no longer worked. I could not work my brain around the connections between those mystifying letter combinations and anything that made sense. It took so much effort to puzzle out each word that by the time I made it to the period, the sentence had no meaning. I could not comprehend, could not even fathom how what I was struggling to piece together had anything to do with the wonderful story-time books Ms. Savage read to us. They were two distinctly separate things-and yet, everyone else seemed to be "getting it."

When, as one by one, the other kids in my "red thin reader" group moved on to thicker books, I began to realize that a) I was different, and b) I was behind. I had never been conscious of either reality before. I felt exactly the way my therapists had feared I would: like I had been thrown into a wolves' den. Way out of my comfort zone, I constantly scrambled to catch up with every assignment in every subject. I wanted to perform, I wanted to be successful, I wanted to be smart; more than anything, I wanted to get to that bigger reader. I tried my best, but those letters and sounds and groupings frustrated me.

No wonder the people at Cedars had recommended I go into a special "day class." They knew I was neither emotionally nor academically prepared for a mainstream environment. If my mom had not fought so virulently for me, the administration would have put me into something like the "Resource Class" I had to attend. It was an hour of nothing every day. We did not learn anything, we did not have fun; we did not do anything! We just sat there. I enjoyed being in class, doing the exercises, and struggling with the words even though it was difficult for me. At least we had a routine: first, we listened to a story, then we broke into reading groups, then we did math, then we did something else, and finally we went to recess. All the while, the Resource Class did nothing. It was like prison: boring and stagnant. Some kids spent their whole day in that class.

Thank you, Mom, for saving me from that fate.

I could not help but notice that the kids in the Resource Class had issues. There was something wrong with them-but why was I there? There was nothing wrong with me. As far as I could tell, I was fine, just another normal, hard-working, well-behaved, attentive student who had a little bit of trouble sounding out words and understanding numbers. I might occasionally pick my nose and do other stuff like that, but I did not hit or bite anymore, and I was definitely out of my shell and looking to interact and connect. Maybe a speech therapist pulled me out of class every week to work on the trouble I had with "th" and a few other sounds, and maybe she continually addressed my eye-contact avoidance issue, but that did not mean I belonged in Resource, staring at the walls all day.

Of course, I was a social outcast. I went to school full of anxiety every day, knowing I would be picked on, teased, bullied, or just plain left out. Every day. Not a day went by that I was left alone. Other kids went through that, too-children are notoriously cruel-but what made me even more different was my reaction: I did not allow it to discourage me. Some of the others who got teased became behavioral problems or class clowns; some shied away and kept to themselves all the time, reading through recess and doing everything alone. I did not want to do that. I wanted friends. I sought attention. I craved being "part of." At recess, I tried to play with the other kids even if they did not want me. I constantly got knocked down, but I kept getting up and coming back for more. I was not masochistic. I was determined.

And I was bucking the tide. At home, my mother still modeled the idea that friends were not important : "Just do your own thing. You're above friends." At school, I inadvertently pushed people away because I still had no social skills, instincts, or clue about how my inappropriate behavior affected other people. I remember wanting this one kid's attention once, so I picked my nose and tried to put the booger on him. Needless to say, he got upset and called for Ms. Savage, who got angry and told me to never do that again, it was very wrong. I instantly earned the nickname "Booger Man" but was never punished at school for that or any of my other transgressions.

At home, my parents would send me to my room, the worst punishment possible. I could not stand it. I would rather be spanked, because it would happen and be over. My parents started putting me in my room when I was a toddler, using a baby gate to keep me in for five or ten minutes while I cried myself into ever greater frustration. As I got older, the gate was replaced by a closed door and the length of confinement grew longer and longer. But this was the age of enforced teacher understanding and reasoning, so Ms. Savage did not even call or send a note home. I got away with just a stern reprimand from my wonderful teacher, leaving me with the same sad, sick-stomach feeling as when I opened Uncle Cary's car door in traffic.

Gym class, or P.E. as they called it, was another problem area for me. For forty-five minutes every day, Coaches Davis and Danny directed us to play capture-the-flag, softball, and other team sports. I was not good at team sports. I was not good at individual sports. I really liked my coaches, but we both knew they could not help me. In fact, they knew —everyone knew-that I had I.E.P.s (Individualized Education Programs), wherein my teachers, the principal, the Special Ed people, and my parents got together every six months to discuss my progress. From their perspective, I was in Special Ed in a mainstream environment until eighth grade. From my perspective, I was on my own. Without a Shelley or another adult standing by me all the time, stopping me from wrongdoing, I had no choice but to figure out by myself how to do it right. If this was a challenge in the classroom, it was an ordeal in P.E.

I was always picked last for the team, always ignored for receiving the ball, always shoved out of the way in every game. P.E. pushed "outcast" up a notch to "pariah." I did not understand why it kept happening. I knew I was different, but that different? I was not like those kids in Resource! I was a good kid: I did my best, I behaved well in class. I was engaged in everything Ms. Savage taught us. So, no matter how many times I got kicked or elbowed aside or sneered at or ignored, I tried again and again. The other kids expected me to give up. The administration expected me to need Resource. My parents expected me to figure it out or just push through. I wanted to be liked-to be "part of," to succeed-so since I could not figure it out, I pushed through. I kept going. What other choice did I have?

My mother's career was back on course by this time, so with both parents working, I went to Roosevelt's after-school daycare program until six o'clock when Dad picked me up. Daycare was easy, like Resource, but much freer. All I had to do was check in and participate in a fifteen-minute group time. After that, everyone pretty much did whatever we wanted for the rest of the afternoon: go outside, read, run around on the playground, play with the blocks, whatever.

Daycare was for first through sixth grade, so it was a tricky environment for me. A lot of the kids were in cliques of friends I could not get into; here, again, I noticed that I was not automatically included as I had been in nursery school and kindergarten. My knee-jerk response was to act out. I knocked over some kid's blocks. I told someone else they were ugly or did something to make them feel bad. Not knowing any other way to attract attention and hurt because I felt excluded, I reverted to nursery-school behavior and unintentionally alienated the very people I wanted to impress.

Eventually, it seeped into my consciousness that I could not get anywhere with the kids in Daycare, so I began hanging out with Ms. Savage in my classroom. She often stayed late preparing for the next day, hanging holiday decorations, or changing the posters around the room. I really liked her. It never occurred to me that being more comfortable around a forty-five, maybe fifty-year-old woman than a kid my own age just made me all the more different.

At the end of our first-grade year, we took a standardized test. When I saw my scores, it finally hit me: I was different. Very different. Suddenly, I knew why none of the other kids liked me: they were smart. I was not.

I was ashamed of myself. I had let down my parents— especially my mom, who had such faith in me, who had fought so hard for me to be in a real class with a real teacher doing real school work instead of in a "day class" or an upgraded kindergarten. Deep inside, I knew I was not like those kids in Resource. I could not do what they did: sit around all day learning nothing and going nowhere. From that point, I did not just want to succeed, I had to succeed-and not just because my mom was counting on me. I knew she was right. I could live up to her expectations. As of now, they were my expectations, too.

Next year, I would work harder and get smarter. That was the only possible answer.

7
Quarter Turn Toward the Right

Autism involves focus to the exclusion of all else. When I flipped those light switches and flushed those toilets, I was so absorbed, so focused, that nothing beyond that occupation existed: not time, not my parents, not even hunger. Once we started having homework and spelling tests in second grade, I began applying that inborn focus to my schoolwork.

I did not do it consciously; that was yet another connection I did not recognize. Nevertheless, I studied two hours a night for those spelling tests. Two hours a night on "my," "any," "will," "have," "you," "might," "it," "important," "beautiful," and "people." And I did it pretty much on my own. My mother worked full-time and my dad was generally tired after a long day at work, so while they would help me if I was really stuck, most of the time they merely said, "Go look it up in the dictionary."

Those test scores had left me feeling inadequate and ashamed. I was not as good or as far along as I thought

55

I should be—as Mom fully expected me to be—so I also could not bring myself to ask my teachers for extra time. They were all wonderful and gave me as much help as they could, but I knew it was all on me. Succeeding became very intimate, very personal, just as my earlier behavior had been for my mother. Feeling the weight of that responsibility, I became intense—just like my mother. I pushed myself to work harder and harder and used my focus "dis"-ability, possibly the only thing I was more advanced at than my peers, to do the best I could with what tools I had. I taught myself to learn. It was a grueling, but powerfully individualistic experience compared to the constant support I had enjoyed at Cedars. Of course, I was only a kid at the time, and none of these psycho-developmental concepts would have made any sense to me. I only knew I felt pressured, lonely, and inadequate, but was going to become the most hardworking, steadfast, and focused person in my school.

My diligence paid off. I became friendly, if not exactly friends, with some of the kids in my class, so I always had someone to play with including two particular boys who let me hang out with them. I still lacked social instincts and skills and teased people for attention, but either these two guys tolerated it better than the rest or they just did not care.

Once when the three of us were on the playground, one of them pulled out a match book. I knew better than to play with matches. I knew they were dangerous. But I also knew these guys did not call me fag or wimp or Booger Man. When the one with the matches said he wanted to light them—"We can do it in the bathroom. There's nothing to burn in the bathroom"—my craving for friendship beat out my better judgment. We all went to the boy's room, where they started lighting the matches. Of course we got caught. Some other student walked into the bathroom, yelled, "Hey! You're not supposed to do that!" and ran to tell the first adult he

56

saw. The next thing I knew, we were being interrogated in Principal Harris's office: "Did you do this? Why did you do this? You boys are in big trouble! Do you realize you could get expelled for this? Now I have to call your parents!"

My stomach was in knots with guilt and fear. Playing with matches was extraordinarily bad, irreversibly horrible—and I had not even done it, which made me feel even sicker. I was caught in the middle, the proverbial witness being tried as a co-conspirator. What was I supposed to do? Rat out my newly acquired friends?!

I only had a few friends; I had to be loyal to them. But then my mom came in, and she and Mr. Harris were both so angry. He kept saying, "You can get kicked out of school!" Trapped, confused, guilty, and frightened, I finally blurted out the name of the boy who had actually lit the matches. The other two of us merely watched. I felt even worse after that for letting my friend down, but somehow I also felt better. The whole episode had an enormous impact on me. I stopped liking the principal, for one thing, and promised myself I would never do anything to upset him or get sent to his office again. For the rest of my elementary-school career, I carefully did not cross certain lines.

By the end of second grade, I had improved enough academically to be put in a third-fourth combination class the following year. The move made me feel vindicated-I was smart!-but it also made for an extremely awkward third-grade term. I felt uncomfortable at school; sometimes, for the first time, I did not even feel safe. My third-grade classmates were eight and nine. The nine and ten-year-old fourth-grade boys were all pretty rough-and-tumble and looked at me as a wimp, an easy punching bag. They would grab my arm and just punch, punch, punch. I never told anyone, but I went home with black-and-blue marks all the time. Just as one set of bruises started to heal, I got another. This kept up all the way through eighth grade. I was such an easy target.

P.E. was a big part of the problem. I still could not play sports. Any sports. A group of boys from my class played basketball with some of the older kids every day after lunch. I just stood and watched. On those rare occasions when they let me in their game, I sucked. With all the pull-out sessions, private therapy, and articulation drills, no one ever helped with me hand-eye coordination, one of my more prominent (to me) developmental delays. I had low muscle-tone and ran tilted. I looked uncoordinated and funny and just assumed I was a failure at basketball, handball, baseball, and all other "ball" activities.

What was wrong with me? Even though they probably did not know what the words meant, it hurt when the other kids called me fag or wimp. I even felt inferior when I was with the few friends I had; I felt as if I was the "also" or "other" instead of an actual "part of." I still teased people, but I was very shy and very, very unaware of how to really make friends rather than be a tag-along. I desperately wanted to belong, to impress people, to become close with other people, so I kept putting myself out there, but it was nerve-wracking for someone so shy. I was embarrassed all the time. Nevertheless, I endured and kept at it. I would not accept any other option.

I was too mortified to go to my parents with any of this. I knew my mom would tell me to forget about making friends, and my dad-well, he coached my T-ball team. How could I tell him I saw the ball over here when it was really over there? It was easier to simply accept that, okay this is me. I suck, I am a failure, and that is the way it is.

Our school district started a GATE (Gifted and Talented Education) program while I was in third grade. Every Wednesday a bus would take those special, hand-picked students to a different school for their special, higher-quality program.

I did not know what the program was all about or even if I would like it, but since a lot of the kids I knew were chosen to go, I wanted to go, too. When I told my mom I had not made the list to be tested; she called my teacher and demanded I be given the chance.

That is how things were back then: it was all about winning, all about being on top. In my kids' generation, everyone gets a trophy, win or lose. That is pretty unrealistic; I am glad I was brought up the way I was. My successes are the result of overcoming a slew of obstacles, one of which was the unspoken-but-nevertheless-virulent belief that if I was not the best, I was a failure. And that was exactly how I felt most of the time: like a failure.

Taking the GATE test only reinforced that perception, because my scores were not up to GATE standards. I was beyond humiliated. I had gone out of my way, demanded and received special treatment, all designed to prove I was smart. Now, I had just proven to everyone that I was not. Could I be more of a failure?

I was so devastated, so beside myself with shame and frustration, that when one of the fourth-grade boys in my third-fourth class said something snide about it, I snapped. Usually, I was careful not to piss off this guy because he was so overall mean to me. He called me names, he tripped me, he sneered at me. He was one of the boys who liked to trap me on the playground and whale away on my arm; I owed a lot of my black-and-blue marks to him. But that day—having degraded myself in front of the whole class, my few friends, my teacher, my parents, and everyone else in my universe—my rage and humiliation somehow turned into courage, and I stood up in the middle of the class and cussed him out, right in front of everyone.

I guess my teacher must have understood what was going on with me; she did not send me to the principal.

8
Successful! But Not

I lived a very adult-focused life during elementary school. I rarely saw any friends after daycare or on weekends. Everything in our house remained centered on our nuclear family in our insulated condominium. Dad often made me dinner when we got home, because Mom was working her tail off. I did some homework, watched some TV—I had one in my room by then-and sometimes played on our Apple II computer. Occasionally, I did not get to my homework until very late. Whenever I did not finish by midnight, I set my alarm for five o'clock in the morning and finished it then.

I excelled in fourth, fifth, and sixth grades. I never made it to GATE, but I was definitely one of the smart kids. Not that that mattered to my classmates. I was still unpopular and still dead weight on any team in P.E. Even the girls would not pick me. In fact, none of the girls liked me; almost of all them totally shunned me. I did not blame them: I teased them even more than I harassed the boys. I was so socially inept. Apparently, one is either born with instincts or not; they do not develop, they do not grow. I had none. Everything I know about dealing with people was learned, usually the hard way.

When I got into fifth and sixth grade, I became more interested in girls, just like every other boy my age, but none of them wanted anything to do with me. My mom, who did not concern herself with friendships in any form, could not help me, and my dad went along with whatever Mom thought as far as I was concerned. Consequently, I spent all my non-school time at home with my parents. We continued our weekend rituals of brunch and grocery shopping on Saturdays and the Santa Monica pier on Sundays, but seldom went anywhere beyond that. When Dad and I went to the 1989 Super Bowl in Miami, Mom stayed home. They went to San Francisco once, but only stayed the weekend. We never took family vacations, my parents never socialized, and we rarely saw my mom's family. They never even went out to dinner together. Our lives were family-centric and work-oriented. This is what life was about, end of discussion.

I wanted more. As time went by, my craving for friends grew. I knew I was separating from my mother in that regard, but I decided my need for more meaningful relationships took priority. My therapist called it individuating, and, as usual, I was a couple years behind in this area. Nevertheless, sometime during fifth grade I occasionally hung out with a friend on the weekend rather than go shopping with my mom and dad, and by sixth grade I had friends who slept over at my house and invited me to sleep over at theirs. They were surprised at first that I had not had "sleepovers" since nursery school, but we got past that pretty quickly.

I kissed my first girl sometime during sixth grade.

I also had a major popularity breakthrough for a short burst of time and got elected to student council. My therapists from Cedars had kept up with my mother all this time, and were so impressed with my transformation that they invited us to that year's pre-school graduation as an inspiration. I was their low-functioning-autistic, slightly retarded, against-all-odds success story.

At least that is how I appeared to the world. I know my mother felt vindicated and maybe even a little bit superior; she had, after all, been the one who insisted I could be mainstreamed and succeed despite all the gloom-and-doom predictions and dire-warning sign posts along the way. My dad was certainly proud; so were Shelley and all my former therapeutic companions and teachers. None of them had any idea that I still huddled alone in my darkened walk-in closet or very small bathroom trying to recapture that sense of peace and comfort I vaguely remembered from what seemed like eons ago. I alone knew that I still purposely avoided looking anyone in the eye because it was too dangerous, or that the very idea of being so vulnerable as to enjoy the intimacy of a "best friend forever" caused me to recoil in panic. In the midst of all those accolades, only I recognized that I still had no life skills whatsoever.

Life skills. Vulnerability. No one had ever talked to me about those concepts. No one ever considered physical therapy to help me overcome my awkwardness or occupational therapy to coach me in social skills. My therapists never expected me to need them, my mother did not think they were important, and my dad—well, he just went along. So there I was at age twelve, a "successful" sixth-grade graduate, an academic high-achiever who worried about every word that came out of his mouth, every gesture he made, every chance meeting with a new person, every glance and expression and passing remark because I had no idea what the heck any of it meant. I no longer displayed any outward signs of autism, but my psychological and emotional "development" remained significantly delayed.

And I told no one.

The summer following sixth grade, I went to sleep-away camp for the first time. My dad drove me up to the camp in Malibu Canyon. Once the parents left, the counselors got everyone situated in their cabins and jumped right in with an orientation-day group activity. I had not even met the other eleven people in my cabin, yet here I was facing twenty strangers who I had to get along with well enough to come up with a symbol or logo for our team. I was lost and bewildered, old feelings I thought I had banished years ago, so I just sat there being homesick, my brain stuck in a loop of, "What am I suppose to do now? How am I gonna make friends?" I went from finally achieving a degree of popularity after working at it for six full years to feeling as if I had returned to ground zero. I was too old to pick my nose, and I did not want to hit or tease anyone. I just wanted to get along, fit in, and maybe, just maybe, make a new friend. But I still could not simply strike up a conversation. How did people do that?

My group worked on the symbol thing for four hours while I watched, too nervous to even talk. What if I said the wrong thing? No one would like me. What if I do one of the activities wrong? People would laugh at and tease me. I was on a coed team at a coed camp, but it did not matter: I was as shy around the boys as the girls. And yet, I was where I wanted to be. I wanted to be social; I wanted to rise to the challenge of making new friends. If only all those people I wanted to be friends with did not scare me to death.

It turned out that other people were nervous, too. Soleil Moon Frye, who was pretty much at the end of her Punky Brewster career, was at the same camp that summer. I had a big crush on her, but, of course, I could not approach her, and had no idea what to say if we met.

She was a little awkward, though; I sensed she was not any more comfortable than I was. For one thing, a lot of people called her Punky, not Soleil, and that put her off. She was also fairly well developed, which seemed to be an issue for her. While I never did figure out how to talk to her, I silently commiserated with her discomfort.

I did not talk to a lot of people. I answered questions, but I could not relax and simply converse with the other kids. I wanted to crawl under a rock by myself whenever somebody wanted to talk to me, so I chose solitary activities—sailing, riflery, horseback riding, motorbike riding—and avoided the group activities as much as I could. I also stalled in the bathroom or the cabin a little longer, minimizing the amount of time I spent with the other campers as much as possible. I even fantasized about how to avoid those situations where everyone got together or did a team sport. When in doubt, I went sailing.

I loved sailing. The instructor worked closely with me at first because, naturally, I did not get it initially. It took me a little longer to pick up on things like tying a figure-eight knot.

Tying had always been a problem for me. I did not tie my own shoes until I was eight, and even then avoided doing it because my fingers did not just do what I wanted them to do. God bless the guy who invented Velcro. I never wore a tie until my middle-school commencement, and luckily, Dad was there to tie it for me. I had no need for a tie after that until I went on an interview the summer before my freshman year of college. Once I got the job, I sometimes had to wear a tie to help the owner pitch business. My dad pre-tied all my ties so I could just slip them over my head and tighten them. I finally figured out how to do it myself; it just took me a little longer, until my sophomore or junior year of college. Still, I always needed some extra, individualized help.

Once I learned how to sail, I went out on Castaic Lake pretty much every day I could during the entire six weeks. The weather was typically around 100 degrees, dry, and with a breeze. I took that boat out by myself and just enjoyed the beautiful lake-what a wonderful feeling! The best feeling in the world. I got really good at sailing. Unlike baseball or basketball, where I had to weave around and with other people, I could set up the boat myself and sail it myself. I could even teach others about it. I loved showing other people things I knew. It made me feel more confident when I taught someone how to put the boat together, put up the sail or attach the rudder. It felt even better that they wanted and accepted my help.

Suddenly, I had a new way to relate to people. Teaching not only gave me a concrete conversational topic, it was fun! It made me feel special and confident, especially since I was so good at it. By the end of the summer, I was sailing 16-foot or 18-foot catamarans, teaching others how to sail them, and sometimes skippering when other campers were on the boat. Yeah, me, the Skipper— what a great feeling! And not simply because I was good at it—the other kids and counselors also knew I was good and respected me for it.

I was good at shooting rifles and pistols, too, which was both surprising and gratifying considering my hand-eye coordination trouble. I had never handled a gun before, but our instructor, a police officer, worked with me one-on-one. I became quite proficient at hitting the target. I loved handling and shooting the gun, loved the loud noise and the excitement of it all. I sent my paper rifle-range targets to my mom inside my letters. I wanted to exhibit my accomplishment and show off my budding independence. I knew she hated any kind of violence, especially guns.

Archery was another thing I could do by myself once I learned how, but it was not as much fun as shooting or sailing. I soon found it boring and returned to the physical challenges of sailing. I went pretty fast in those boats when we got a good wind. Sometimes I capsized the boat, but that was fun, too.

When not sailing or shooting, I kept myself busy with other individualized sports. I went horseback riding and rode motorbikes across the dirt paths. I pretty much did anything and everything I could to be alone and not have to interact with the other kids because I quickly developed the same kind of problems with my cabin mates that I had in school. They responded to my shyness and social awkwardness with the same name calling: fag, wimp, stuff like that. It was strange, as if those words were printed across my forehead. This was the 1980s, when you were either cool or not cool. If you were not cool, people called you a fag or a wimp. Not a nerd or a jerk or a geek; those words came from other eras. In the 1980s, homophobia and the AIDS crisis were at their peaks, so fag and wimp carried a lot of negative power and projected hurt.

I spent six weeks at camp and wrote my parents every day. The mail typically came around four or five o'clock, just about the time we got back from the day's activities, and I always had a letter from my mom. Except for when I went sailing, that was my favorite time of day. Her letters helped me get through the nights, when we had different types of group activities like cooking s'mores at the beach and other typical camp things. I could not avoid being with the other kids so much, so I did the best I could under the circumstances. I shadowed my "cool" cabin mates, even if they picked on me, so I could look "cool," too. I did not fool anyone, but what else could I do? Other people's opinions had become very important to me.

I got home from camp and spent the rest of the summer at the beach or hanging around our complex's pool. It was a let-down from camp, but the weeks passed, and I felt pretty good about myself as I faced the new school year in a new school.

And then I went to junior high, and the walls crumbled down around me.

9
Down Again

Lincoln Middle School went from sixth through eighth grade, but I started my junior-high experience as a seventh grader because our class was the last one at Roosevelt Elementary to graduate at the end of sixth grade instead of fifth. Everyone from Roosevelt went to Lincoln, but since several other schools also fed into the middle school, I once again faced meeting a lot of new people. I also had to deal with the totally new and overwhelming routine of moving between classrooms and different teachers every period. As if that wasn't intimidating enough, I was also scared to death due to rumors we heard at Roosevelt that the bigger or older Lincoln kids' favorite prank was "trashing": they literally threw people into the trash dumpster. I did not get beaten up as much anymore at Roosevelt, and I did not want to return to being hyper-vigilant every minute of the day. My only saving grace was starting Lincoln in the middle of the three grades. I wasn't one of the youngest or smallest in the school. Unfortunately, my recent academic success worked against me when we all moved to middle school, because my friends went one way and I was sent another.

The school divided our giant incoming class into "cores." I was in the Gold core and all my friends, especially my good friends with whom I had sleepovers, were in the Green core. Each core went to classes together, and all the cores were on slightly different schedules, so even before school started I knew I could not hang out with my support-system friends or rely on them to stand up for me. I might not even see them at all during the school day. I was twelve, pudgy, and launching into puberty, and my mom's life-long affectionate nickname for me, Tubby, rankled me. She was in no mood to drop her favorite nickname, though; I think it came from her own memories of the Mickey Mouse Club.

That first day of middle school made my first day of camp seem easy. I was incredibly nervous the whole day: what would I do for recess? Who would I sit with at lunch? What would P.E. be like?

I was really in a bad place with too many levels of unfamiliar and scary stuff going on. Diagnosed with Lupus, Mom was hospitalized practically every month and spent most of her time at home in bed. She still worked a little, but the pain made it progressively harder for her to keep up with her own life, let alone mine. We had not gotten along for years; now our relationship became just that much worse. I hung out with my friends after school and on weekends, but mostly I was alone with no one to talk to. Dad was too busy and too worried about his wife to deal with my problems. I saw a psychologist once a week because Mom thought I needed someone to help me through all these transitions, but we just talked about the strain between her and me. I was very angry, very scared, and very unhappy with nothing to look forward to except maybe having a weekend sleepover. Everything else in my life just sucked.

We had to suit up for P.E., something else I had not dealt with in elementary school. We stripped down and stored our clothes in lockers—lockers that closed on me and were swung to hit me in the head. It was a living nightmare. I got rat-tailed—snapped with a towel-almost every day. I had never enjoyed P.E. before; now I actively hated it. I remember a swimming session when one of the kids started dunking me. I was a good swimmer, but he kept pushing me under the water again and again without giving me any time to catch my breath. No one saw it or did anything about it if they did see it. I literally thought I was going to die. This was my life day after day.

I hated lunch, too. As I feared, my friends were on a different schedule, so I always sat alone and got teased for it. After I ate, I had nothing to do. Roosevelt had a single basketball court, and I could join or at least watch the game. Lincoln had tons of courts, and no one let me play on any of them. I felt like I was back in first grade. The campus was big and spread out, though, so at least I could escape to the library, the track, or wherever else I could find a hidey hole. Part of me did not want to hide because I had become a social being, but another part— a bigger part—craved safety.

One day, I just got fed up with it all. I woke up upset and simply did not want go to school. I was not sick; I had just had it. Everything, every day was so hard. I felt constantly bombarded with situations and emotions I did not understand and with which I did not know how to cope. The strain of trying to be "normal" and "fit in" was exhausting. It was four miles to school on my bike- I wanted my parents to drive me, but they refused-and the thought of climbing on my bicycle and peddling to a place that filled me with dread sapped my last shred of mental and emotional strength.

I left our apartment as usual and went down to the subterranean garage. We had some storage lockers off to the side-cold, empty, dark spaces where I could slip inside and not be seen. I plunked myself down in one and spent the entire school day there, doing nothing. Just sitting. Waiting for the day to go by. I was done, used up. Between all the physical-growth changes and the horrors of middle school, I had no more fight left in me. I was overwrought and wrung out. That, too, was a big change, because I had been a fighter since I first left Cedars. I went to school every day, bore the brunt of it all, and tried to make it better. But I could feel the emptiness inside, and I had nothing left to stand off the bullies with. I never learned to defend myself physically; my dad never showed me and my mom would have been appalled at the idea. I never had any choice but to bear up, push through, take the abuse, and move on. But not that day. That day, I had no "bear up" or "push through" left.

I sat on that concrete floor all day long being angry and exhausted—and bored stiff. It was the longest seven hours of my life. I might have been back in my elementary school Resource class, except I did not come out for recess, lunch, or even to take a bathroom break. I used to wish I could escape to a small enclosed room, but now that I had, it was nothing like I fantasized. It was too late for me to return to that private, hyper-focused world in which I could do nothing or the same something for hours on end. Those times were over—and that made me feel even more defeated.

When the school day was over, I went upstairs and I told my parents. I guess I expected they would value my honesty and write a note excusing me for the day, but they refused. Instead, they called the school, reported me to the vice principal, and grounded me. This further lack of support—by now, I was sure my parents did not love or care about me—made me even more depressed. They did not even try to understand why I hid, why I felt I had no choice but to hide.

Of course, I never told them anything about what happened at school, so they had no way of understanding what was going on with me, but that is the adult in me talking, not the budding teenager who felt abused, belittled, rejected, and abandoned. My parents did not know that I still could not approach new people or make new friends. They had no clue as to the physical, mental, and emotional abuse I absorbed every day. I had never let them know that school was a constant battle for which I had no armor, no weapons, and no backup.

The vice principal gave me detention every day after school for a couple weeks plus two Saturday sessions from eight in the morning until two in the afternoon. The Breakfast Club was nothing compared to our Saturday detention. We were not confined to sitting in the library. We had to scrape gum off the concrete, paint over graffiti, and do other extremely not-fun stuff. We also had to write an essay about why we were there. I wrote, "I never want to do this again."

I got a lot of other detention that year, too.

My science teacher, Mr. Pitcher, was one of those instructors who did not have a lot of control over his class. I later learned he was a great teacher, but for most of the year, I only knew that people acted up in his class all the time. My mind said, "Ah ha! A new outlet for getting attention!" I made jokes and played the class clown, figuring my obnoxiousness would get me favored by my peers and maybe, somehow, convert some of them into new friends. I had no idea how that would happen, but I was so hyper-focused on the idea that I went out of my way to crack more jokes than anyone else and interrupt the class as much as I possibly could. In turn, Mr. Pitcher gave me detention almost every other week or sent me to the vice principal, never a good experience. Some part of my mind connected those dots between what I did and the punishments I endured, but with so much going wrong in my life all at once, I disregarded those flimsy correlations and instead wallowed in feeling misunderstood, abandoned, and alone.

I did not waste my psychologist's time talking about any of this. Our conversations always centered on my frustrations with my mom. He told me to open up and tell her what was bothering me, but I never got a good reception with that. Mom did not listen to me. A lot of teenagers think that about their parents, but in this case, it was fact, not perception. She did not listen. She would not listen—and she would say so, too. She was not interested in anything I had to say. She was always like that, even before she got sick, because she always believed she was right about everything. She knew best no matter what, and that was that. Being so strong-willed probably got her through her illness, but that illness effectively erased any patience she previously had, although I have trouble thinking of Mom and the word "patience" together. She never really had any; she was too dynamic, too successful, too driven for that kind of attribute. Here was a beautiful woman struck down not only in the prime of her life, but also in the prime of her career, which was absolutely critical to her. She was not really "open" to discussions. Mostly, she was angry. So was I—but she had little tolerance for my anger, ongoing social problems, or the developmental issues I still struggled with because as far as she was concerned, I either had or should have outgrown all that by now. And since she was always right, there was simply nowhere to go with that.

There was nowhere to go as far as getting adult help at school either. This was before people realized the dangers of bullying, before the hallway cameras, on-campus security guards, teacher/administration sensitivity training. No adult at Lincoln ever noticed what went on with me or with any of the other kids being picked on. Telling only made the situation worse. No one was there to protect us in those days. Every kid was pretty much on their own.

I know I certainly was.

10
Theater to the Rescue

I spent most of seventh grade as a behavioral problem for the school authorities and an academic let-down for my parents. I did not live up to anyone's expectations, including my own. My grades dropped to all Cs in science, math, English, and geography, but for the first time in my life, I did not care. I made a complete 180-degree turn toward the negative.

As part of my new self-destructive track, I persuaded my local liquor store to sell me cigarettes, which I smoked with my friends. I could not bring myself to inhale, but I looked cool. Rather than slave over homework or study for tests, I hung out and played video games at the arcade. Fortunately, I never got involved with drugs, but I set myself up to fail all around. If the counselors in my new school were monitoring me—and with my history, they most likely were—they undoubtedly thought my elementary-school success had been a fluke and that

I was about to prove no one simply "overcomes" autism.

Toward the end of the school year, all seventh graders had to pick a short-term elective. I could opt for a language or something else academically oriented, but instead, I chose stage crew because it looked interesting and easy. Stage crew was run by Mr. Pitcher, the science teacher in whose class I had elevated obnoxious to an art form. I could not blame him if he hated me, which I thought he did. But stage crew changed all that.

Our relatively new junior-high theater held 500 people. The school district rented it out to groups for amateur productions and other events and hired fourteen-year-old stage-crew students to open up the auditorium and manage the property. A custodian was always on the grounds, but he usually disappeared into his office, leaving the students to handle the lighting and sound equipment, supervise the auditorium, and generally make sure no one did something they should not do. The students essentially represented the district.

As soon as I heard about the job, I wanted it.

I learned how to run the lights and sound system. I learned to go up on the catwalks, how to handle scenery and curtain cues, and how to work all the other backstage mechanics that make a show run smoothly. I have no idea how the district handled the liability issue-I doubt kids are allowed to do those kinds of things today-but we students ran the theater. The more I learned, the more I enjoyed everything about stage crew and its potential. I shook off my negativity and slipped back toward my amiable, polite nature. As a result, Mr. Pitcher willingly gave me the extra time I still always needed. Stage crew was responsible for my turnaround. I discovered the joys and appeal of running things behind the scenes, developed a new goal, and acquired a thirst for adult responsibilities.

When I went back to camp that summer, I had an upbeat sense of expectation. I remembered some of the people and already knew what to expect, so I was far more comfortable and excited, and consequently had a better time from the onset. I got so much better at sailing that the instructors had me assist them almost every day. I even began making friends.

I befriended fourteen-year-old Becky when she came down to the dock to go sailing. She was a year older than me and really cute. She had never sailed before, so I helped her, and just like that, we jetted off together on a catamaran. I never managed to reproduce that kind of instant connection.

We spent a lot of time together and I really liked her, but I still lacked social skills and instincts, so I did not recognize her cues and consequently did not know what to do with or about her. Of course, a good part of that ignorance was probably normal for a thirteen-year-old going through puberty.

As teen campers, we got to stay up later and watch movies while the rest of the camp went to bed. One awesome night, she and I sat together watching *The Lost Boys*. Everything felt so good. I really wanted to kiss her, but I did not know how. I wanted to put my arm around her, but could not do that either. I was too shy to even hold her hand. We went our separate ways after camp, but not before I realized how much I liked hanging out with girls. I felt a bond with Becky even though everything was strictly platonic. She was soft and non-judgmental and very kind. I felt more equal to her than I did with most people, as if I did not have to compete or impress her after a certain point. I experienced a level of comfort I had not known in years. I had never realized that girls could be potential friends. They always stayed away from me-and, as with Mr. Pitcher, I could not blame them. I only knew to tease them.

Jenny was a perfect example. I teased the hell out of her back in sixth grade because I liked her so much. Once, I asked her out in a playful way and then told people we were dating. It was a lie; I never went anywhere with anyone. Not surprisingly, she did not appreciate the rumors I spread. One night, I called our local radio station and dedicated Toto's "I'll be Over You" to her. I had no idea what the song meant; I never even listened to the lyrics. When the DJ said, "Oh, did Jenny break up with you?" I responded, "No, I broke up with her." They played the entire interchange on the radio, and I taped it, so proud of myself. The next day, I played the tape for everyone at school to show off. It never occurred to me that my prank might hurt Jenny. I reconnected with Jenny on Facebook a few years ago; luckily, she has forgotten the entire incident.

Between Jenny in sixth grade and my camp friend Becky the summer before eighth grade, I had no relationships with any female other than my mother. Spending time with Becky made me realize that girls were people, not just glam-rock poster decorations, and that my mom was not necessarily typical of the gender. Mom was not comforting or calm most of the time. Or soft—definitely not soft. But other girls were.

I came back from summer camp about twenty pounds thinner and a foot taller. With my baby fat gone, I was more confident and comfortable than I had ever been before. And I wanted that theater job! I decided to make a fresh start come the new school year, and decided to go back to being a good student. I wanted Mr. Pitcher to trust me enough to hire me as soon as I turned fourteen.

That Fall, 1988, we held a mock election between George Bush and Michael Dukakis. As one of only a handful of Republicans in the school, I was selected to be George Bush. I spent a month giving speeches, putting up campaign posters, and getting ready for the big debate in front of the whole school, which was followed by our own "election."

For years, I had watched CNN, read the newspaper,

and discussed politics with my friend Eric. That fall, I spent my afternoons volunteering at the Republican headquarters in Santa Monica. I enjoyed working with the adults; I related to them much easier than to kids my own age. They considered me a novelty because I sounded so adult-like for a thirteen-year-old. Working on something important like the election made me feel special, almost as if I was above those kids who still gave me a hard time. Consequently, I felt pretty confident by the time we got to the school debate in school, and I did a good job even though it was my first time speaking in public. I was as eloquent as a thirteen year old can be, especially since I had been explaining "my" platform on the phone and to walk-ins at GOP headquarters for several months. Despite my persuasive arguments, though, the mostly Democratic student population elected Dukakis.

Despite my failure at the mock polls, I came through the episode with a new focus based on a collection of discoveries. For one, my brief foray into politics introduced me to how adults really worked, independently and together. I liked it. I also discovered that working was more enjoyable than anything I had ever done. I learned more important things than the stuff they taught in school, and the feeling of involvement, of being "part of," satisfied that craving I had felt since first grade. I began developing a new set of expectations for myself. I could not articulate them at that point, but somewhere deep inside I knew I had rounded some kind of corner.

I turned over a new leaf. I never again got detention or acted out in class. I did my homework on time, and my grades went back up. The only thing that ran a little amuck that year was my first sexual experience. Neither of us was ready for it, but it happened anyway.

Martin Luther King Day, 1989 was a school holiday, so a bunch of people were at my friend Joe's house playing Truth or Dare. One was a girl who liked me a lot. She was not all that cute, but she had come out of nowhere at the end of seventh grade, signed my yearbook, and given me a big hug. Ours was a big school; I did not even know who she was. We ended up in some class together in eighth grade, and somehow began talking on the phone every night, which was a lot of fun since we some-how always got to talking about sex and what we wanted to do with/to each other. Neither of us had any experi-ence whatsoever or understood a thing we were saying. We were just having fun—until Martin Luther King Day.

Joe dared her to perform oral sex on me. I have no idea why; I did not put him up to it. She said yes, which shocked everyone, especially me. I probably ejaculated in less than ten seconds; it was a wonderfully powerful sensation, especially for someone who had never even masturbated before.

Everything immediately got awkward, both then and the next day at school, when rumors started to spread. Next thing I know, I was in the counselor's office. The girl had told him what happened. He called me in for questioning, and I told him the same story. We both got lectured about sex. Afterward, the counselor said he had to call our parents. I asked, "Can I talk to them about it first?" Surprisingly, he said yes. The girl had already called her parents, a very nice Persian couple who came in that day. They took me into a private office. I felt like scum.

"We don't want our daughter doing that."

"I know."

It reads so easy on paper, but the whole thing was se-riously traumatic on so many levels. I went right home after school and told my parents.

Amazingly, my mom was okay with it. She did not want me doing it again, but whenever it came to adult things like that, she was mind-bogglingly supportive and nonjudgmental. My older, Southern-conservative dad, on the other hand, got up in arms about the whole thing because it embarrassed him. He never spoke of it to me again. After the flurry died down at school about a week later, no one there brought it up again either. We were all too embarrassed; for once, I felt the same way everyone else did.

About six weeks later when I turned fourteen, Mr. Pitcher hired me to work in the theater.

EMPLOYEE NAME		SCHOOL DISTRICT OF LOS ANGELES COUNTY					LOCATION	SOCIAL SECURITY NUMBER					
HALL, JOHN R		SANTA MONICA-MALIBU UNIFIED*					018		E E D D				
EMPLOYEE STATEMENT OF EARNINGS						PER NO. CYCLE	800 14	PERIOD 12-01-88 TO 12-31-88				ISSUE DATE 01-10-8	
THIS PERIOD YEAR TO DATE	GROSS EARNINGS 78.63 78.63	TAXABLE EARNINGS 78.63 78.63	FEDERAL TAXES	STATE TAXES	O.A.S.D.H.I.		RETIREMENT		VOLUNTARY DEDUCTIONS	E.S.A.	NET PAY 78.6		
ASSIGNMENT NUMBER	C/R BASIS TYPE	RET. CODE	SALARY RATE	PERCENT ASSIGNMENT	TIME UNITS/AMOUNT	AMOUNT EARNED	PAY CODE	VOLUNTARY DEDUCTIONS AND ADJUSTMENTS			EMPLOYER CONTRIBUTIONS		
293353	NHC	26	4.250		18.500	78.63	R						

NOT NEGOTIABLE

6330141   1651 16TH ST, SANTA MONICA, CA, 90404

*ADDRESS

11
New Again and Again

I loved my job in the theater, and I got along well
with the clients using the space. Santa Monica had
an almost-communist version of rent control at the
time, so a Landlords' Rights group met in our auditorium the third Monday of every month. I let them in and
stayed to lock up after they left. The leader of the group
was an older gentleman who smoked like a chimney.
Here I was, a fourteen-year-old kid, having to tell him,
"Sir, you have to put that out!" every month when he lit
up on the stage. One night, when he just would not stop
smoking in the facility, I had to get rather firm with him.
It felt good; I liked being in charge and was proud of the
way I handled my new adult-like position of authority. I
even had the keys to the theater. I took the job very seriously; my friends wanted to hang out there, but I never
let anything like that happen. I put in fifteen to twenty
hours a week at $4.25 an hour. The experience gave me
confidence and made my parents proud. Once, a group

came in to do a production called Dear Mr. Caterer. They were there for an entire month, which meant a lot of extra work time—so much, in fact, that Dad had to bring me roast-beef sandwiches from Izzy's Deli while I did my homework, because I could not make it home for dinner.

I enjoyed my first real taste of independence. I rode my bike everywhere, took the bus, and worked a real job. Life was good. I befriended so many of the people on Dear Mr. Caterer that they invited me to the post-production party. It crept into my mind that I really was more comfortable around adults than with kids my own age. In fact, I was more comfortable working than doing anything else. I liked having a higher purpose to my life than just going to school. It not only helped my self-esteem, it also made me feel "part of" without feeling vulnerable. Work gave me connection without intimacy. What could be more perfect?

School became an issue again anyway, because my mom did not think Santa Monica High School, where most of the kids from Lincoln went next, would be rigorous enough for me. As usual, she thought I could do more than anyone else thought I could. This time I agreed with her, so my parents and I went to a number of private high schools to look around the campuses. I applied to them all, but I had my heart set on Brentwood School with its big, sprawling campus and conservative ambience. It felt like my type of place. As it turned out, Brentwood was the only school that rejected me. My scores on the eighth-grade standardized tests, the SSATs, were too low, and my seventh-grade performance had marred my GPA. Their rejection letter showed up on a Friday afternoon, which bummed me out for the weekend, especially since I also received an acceptance letter from Windward School in the same mail delivery.

I did not want to go to Windward. It was a much smaller school than Brentwood. The main building had only one floor, which was probably no more than 30,000 square feet. The ancillary building on the other side of a flood-control channel was even smaller. Windward took a "progressive" approach to education. A good number of students-not the majority, but a good number-were counter-culture types. Here I was, a clean-cut, Republican, All-American beach kid, about to go to a college-prep high school where people wore tie-dyed clothes and half the guys sported long hair. But Harvard School was an all-boys school at the time, and Brentwood turned me down, so I told myself, "Okay, if I have to go to private school, I'm gonna go to Windward."

Our eighth-grade commencement was once again very emotional for me. I wore a tie for the first time and received a school-district award for Most Improved Student. The whole school-the whole audience-applauded for me. For the first time, I felt engulfed by love and popularity from a large community, not just a little group of one-on-one counselors who praised every kid for every little achievement. It felt good; I still have that award.

That summer, I went to Gold Arrow Camp, located in the mountains northeast of Fresno by Huntington Lake. After the high of graduation, it was disheartening to plummet into yet another unfamiliar situation where I had no friends or comfort and consequently felt alone and out-of-place. I guess I still came across as different even with all the progress I had made, because I was still the one the other boys singled out to pick on and be jerks to the entire first month of camp. The last week of July, our age group went on a five-day survival-training trip up the mountain. We carried all our food and water in our backpacks. Cell phones were not yet commonplace, and we had no radios with which to keep in touch-we were alone out there, totally cut off from the rest of the camp. We hiked into the wilderness at one end of a sixty-mile trail and popped out five days later at the other end.

That hike was one of the most beautiful experiences

of my life. I had never seen natural running water before or the open-air splendor of the mountains. It was pretty much a solitary enjoyment, though, because I had not managed to make any friends with the other kids. As usual, I was alone in the midst of the crowd. It was also hard on me physically because, like everyone else, I carried a seventy-pound backpack around for five days, a major accomplishment for someone who was not used to that level of physical activity. At one point, I thought I had gotten absurdly tired because my backpack felt extraordinarily heavy-which, in fact, it was. A few of the jerks thought it would be real funny to stuff a bunch of rocks in my pack, and I spent half the day lugging eighty pounds around on my back. They all had a good laugh when I discovered the rocks that evening. The counselors yelled at them for the prank, but that was it; they paid no real consequences. I went to sleep wishing I could grow up faster so I did not have to deal with oafs like this anymore and could spend my days with adults like the ones in the GOP and at the theater.

Fortunately, that entire bunch of kids left at the end of that week while I stayed on for two more weeks. The new session was great. Having been at camp for four weeks and now familiar and comfortable with my sur-roundings and routines, I readily made friends with the new campers. Plus, I could show them around, help them get situated, and be something of a cabin leader. I always did better standing confidently out in front than when engulfed by potentially hostile strangers.

Sailing wasn't as much fun as it had been at Castaic, although I did participate in a regatta on Huntington Lake. Even with the new crowd those last two weeks, I still found myself sticking to mostly individual activities where I could be safely alone. I was almost relieved by the time I went home—but then summer ended, and I started another new school.

Public high schools usually run from ninth through

twelfth grade; Windward ran from seventh through twelfth. Consequently, I started a new school in the middle for the second time, with most of my fellow "Freshmen" students already familiar with the grounds, the routines, the teachers, and, of course, each other. This time, however, instead of facing a massive number of unfamiliar faces on a vast campus where I could hide myself away, I confronted a total-school enrollment smaller than the size of my middle-school class. There were only forty-five kids in my whole grade. I was familiar with thirty-student classrooms; Windward's classes had no more than ten students. Since leaving Cedars' programs, I had always called my teachers by their surnames as a matter of respect; here, the students called the teachers by their first names as if to accentuate the school's informality.

I absolutely freaked out that first day at Windward. I knew no one. Everyone else was part of one clique or another, all formed two years earlier. To hide, I escaped into the field beyond the flood-control channel between the main school building and the auxiliary building. At fourteen in a class of fourteen and fifteen year olds, I not only was the new kid, I had an aura of being different that drew mockery like a magnet. And while no one got physically rough, a respite from what I had to contend with in elementary and middle school, boys that age engage by teasing and horsing around. I responded by smiling a lot; I had not yet learned any other coping mechanism.

My first class of the day was Drama, an elective foisted on me possibly because of my stage crew experience. The only relationship between the two pursuits is the involvement of a stage, but that must have been enough of a connection for the powers-that-be to add it to my schedule. Then again, maybe someone thought it would help me get over my shyness. Whatever the reason, the plan backfired. After working at my middle-school theater, I almost laughed at their concept of a "stage". It was in a little auditorium, which was essentially just a large black room. Linsel, a big, burly class-clown kind of guy, yelled "Norm!" every day when he came into class, as if he was walking into Cheers. Everyone played along with him, even the teacher. With just ten kids in the class, there was almost no structure; everyone pretty much did their own thing. After Roosevelt and Lincoln, I felt as if I had been dropped into a foreign land. It was shocking in every which way.

I went from class to class-the school was so small, I could not possibly get lost-and although the teachers were all pleasant enough, I could tell the coursework would be challenging. I looked forward to burying myself in schoolwork, especially when lunch came around, and I was completely alone. No one even looked my way. That first lunch period was the longest thirty minutes of my life. I used the time to discover the field and its secret hiding places.

My nemesis, P.E., was my last class of the day. I dreaded even suiting up amongst all these strangers, but a gentleman named Coach Christian came in to talk to us instead. He was recruiting for the cross-country team. "If you join, you don't have to take P.E. You get a free period."

That was enough for me. I hated P.E., and I loved the idea of a free period. I immediately stuck up my hand and signed on for cross-country.

My first week was absolutely miserable. Hiking with eighty pounds on my back was a walk in the park compared to the first day of track practice. Christian made us run three miles-the first day! I hated running. In junior high we had to run a mile lap once a month and I was terrible at it. In my hurry to avoid gym class and enjoy a free period, I did not connect the dots that "cross-country team" meant running, running, and more running. I wanted to kick myself; even more, I wanted to quit that first day. But I had my mother's determination and my father's fortitude, so I stuck with it. After all, running was still better than P.E., with its endless team games and locker-room embarrassment. Besides, I got pretty good at it in a few weeks. I might not have been the fastest guy on the team, but I found I really loved it. I soon found myself running three or four miles a day even when I didn't have practice. More than just a solitary pursuit, it was a fantastic high. It put me into my comfort zone, that peaceful, totally focused world disconnected from time and outside influences.

The weather in Los Angeles that Fall, 1989, was hot and smoggy. We ran in the San Fernando and San Gabriel Valleys, which were even smoggier, and had our league meets at the Rose Bowl in Pasadena, the ultimate hot, smoggy town at the bottom of the San Gabriel mountains. Cross-country is less about competition and more about going for a personal best time, so once I got into the feel of the pursuit, it was perfect for me. Our first meet at Mount Sac College was my turning point. The campus is extremely hilly and the day was particularly hot; halfway through the race, I thought I was going to die. Rather than give up, though, I pushed on and reaped the awesome payoff that comes with finishing something so arduous. After that race, running became the best part of my day, our meets the one thing I looked forward to as I went from class to class.

Despite that daily respite, my first month or so at Windward proved just as difficult as the one in seventh grade. Some things had not changed: I still did not feel safe meeting people's eyes. I still craved attention and affection but could not make friends until I had been in a place or situation long enough to feel secure. Groups continued to disconcert me. Drama was the perfect example. With only ten people in the class, I had nowhere to hide, no way to avoid learning and performing lines. But with my lack of eye contact and my ubiquitous

91

nervous little cough, I managed to spend most of the class observing rather than participating. I do not think anyone felt cheated when I did not perform. I got pretty good at doing whatever was necessary to get from point A to point B, but I remained so nervous and unaware of what to do beyond memorize and recite that when someone talked to me-and I think the other boys made an early effort to befriend me-I just left. When I couldn't leave, I smiled. It wasn't a blooming-with-happiness smile, it was an I-don't-know-how-to-respond-to-you smile, but I did it so much I earned the nickname Smiley.

I went to one party that September. Matt Shire, Talia Shire's son, asked me to his birthday party in Bel Air. I remembered Talia as the sister who got married in beginning of The Godfather, but I think most people remember her as Adrianne, the girlfriend in Rocky. Anyway, I was excited to go, even though I knew I was only invited because they included everyone in our ninth-grade class. I was also very nervous, of course, because I still did not know how to make small talk or enjoy lighthearted fun. The party was just like school: I felt uncomfortable and out of place, so I barely talked to anyone.

After a few weeks of not relating to the boys in my class-and ninth-grade boys are neither the most forgiving nor welcoming bunch in the world-I decided to shed my outwardly nervous attitude and replace it with protective arrogance: You know what? I don't need these kids, I've got friends at home in Santa Monica. I'm just going to school here. I don't care. I'm above these kids. I cannot remember what good I thought this would do, but I ignored everyone's overtures of friendship, refused to attend any more of their parties, and generally did whatever I could to alienate them. As a result, I took my usual bad situation and made it ten times worse. Instead of sliding by as the intriguing new kid, I turned myself into a pariah. I did not really think I was better than anyone, but it took too much psychological energy to break through to new batch of kids. As I saw it, we were polar opposites of each other: they were comfortable, I was nervous. They were connected, I felt estranged. They were perfectly at home in Windward's liberal, casual milieu; I found myself missing the bells between classes, the formality between teachers and students, and the concrete parameters of assignments and expectations. Nothing in those first few weeks of high school made any sense to me, except running, which, in and of itself, did not really make sense as something I would normally enjoy.

After school and on weekends, I retreated to my comfort zone and hung out with my old friends from elementary school. We all lived in the same area in Santa Monica, and we still smoked together and slept over at each other's houses. We also got into trouble together, because we would leave wherever we were in the middle of the night to buy cigarettes or just wander around Santa Monica. We were not a gang per se, just a group of ninth graders who liked to roam the streets after dark. One night when we were hanging out at our old elementary school, some guys from a real gang jumped us. I recognized one of them; we had been playmates back in first grade. Now he ran with a crowd that beat up stray kids for kicks. They beat us up pretty badly. We almost got stabbed, but we managed to escape by splitting up and running off in different directions. I think that was the last time we hung out at Roosevelt.

Six weeks into the semester, all forty-five ninth graders went on a "block," a week-long retreat to give everyone the chance to bond with each other. I dreaded the very idea. How could I bond with people with whom I shared nothing in common? They took us up to Big Bear where we did camp-like group activities all day, every day. Fortunately, the teachers put us into groups instead of letting the students pick their teams. That helped a little; at least I did not have to stand there and wait, knowing everyone was trying to avoid picking me. Some of the stuff we did turned out to be a lot of fun; the rest I just "got through" the way I had gotten through elementary and middle school. And while I cannot say I actually bonded with anyone, the block did pull me out of my "pariah" status, and I managed to come home with a few new friends. It was the fastest I had ever gone from outcast to "part of" in my life.

12
I'm In!

As the French proverb promises, "One meets his destiny often on the road he takes to avoid it." I was accepted into my first clique in Big Bear. Once we got home, I hung out with them as much as possible. If they fooled around, I fooled around. If they did something I did not want to do or was not good at—I did it anyway. They looked for me to join them, and I was not about to let personal interests stand in my way.

It turned out that for all their outward appearances, most of the people in school were apolitical. They were just into being kids; they did not follow the papers the way I did or watch CNN religiously; they had no interest in who ran for what office or what was happening on the other side of the world. All they cared about was letting loose after school and on the weekends and having some fun.

One of the guys had an undercover police car from a CHP auction. It still had the antennae on the back and the lights on the sides, so it looked like a real police car. He hated driving it, so I mostly drove when we cruised around Hollywood. Some other friends followed us in another car with a video camera. We would cruise by the areas where prostitutes hung out and watch them scatter when they saw our car. Sometimes we waited until one of the girls got picked up and then followed them to their hotel.

Amazingly, we never got into trouble, not even when we did really crazy stuff. I used to drive my mom's Jaguar because I did not have a car of my own and my dad did not like me to use his Mercedes. Once when I stopped for a red light on Sunset Boulevard, the guys in the back seat set off a firecracker! Everybody had to jump out of the car in the middle of the street.

I did not mind them playing those kinds of pranks on me; they were always good natured and harmless and made me feel part of the group. It was such a different paradigm from my earlier friend associations. We were all teenagers just having fun, and I was included as a matter of course because I was part of the group-and usually the one driving. That was part of my contribution to the group: I acted and sounded older and knew how to drive, so I was a valuable asset to keep around.

I knew how to drive because I had been joy-riding in our complex for years. I felt stifled sitting at home with my sick mother and older father on weekends and summer nights, so when I did not stay over at a friend's place, I left our condo around 11:00 PM to work out in the gym or use the billiards room. My parents were okay with that because they knew I was still safely in the building, which had twenty-four hour security guards. What they did not know was that I had I befriended all those security guards, as well as all the valet parking attendants.

Our building had 317 units, and the valet guys kept everybody's car keys on a wall right off the lobby. They would pull a tenant's car out in front whenever someone wanted to go out, and they would let me pick any available set of keys I wanted and take the car out for a spin. What a rush! Most of the time, I just drove around our multi-level garage, but sometimes I went out into the community. The tenants were all very well off, so I got to joy ride in their Mercedes, Cadillacs, Jaguars, and BMWs. Now and then, one of my friends rode along with me. Sometimes, we even had a security guard go out with us. Once when I wanted to go out in a Porsche but did not know how to drive a stick shift, one of the security guards grabbed the keys and we went out together. It was fun until he went crazy behind the wheel. He had his foot plastered to the floor at 100 mph, screaming around corners, bouncing all over the place. I thought we were going to get killed.

Another time, I was driving somebody's Mustang when I accidentally bumped the fender—not horribly, just hard enough to damage it a little bit. I parked the car and walked away, and I was a little more careful with the next car. I was just trying to be a kid, a normal young teenager. My home life was so solemn and my school life so fraught with pitfalls—even just driving around the parking structure was fun. It made me feel free and special, and I treasured it.

One Friday night about a week or so after the 1992 Los Angeles riots, I was driving my friend's police car when the guys in the backseat decided to set off another firecracker. This time, though, an officer heard the thing go off, spun his car around, and pulled us over—at gunpoint! Up to that moment, none of us really appreciated how much the riots had affected life in Los Angeles. He did not arrest us, but he did give us a healthy lecture about how sensitive things were on the streets. People were still taking shots at cops in certain neighborhoods.

"You might wanna be a little more careful driving around in this car. People are shooting at us, they will shoot at you."

I know that happened on a Friday night because we were always tired the next morning when we had to hustle to get down to Torrance for jiu-jitsu lessons. Several of my friends took jiu-jitsu, so I did, too. I was terrible at it, but I did not care. I was part of the clique.

The drive down to Torrance was pretty easy, but we sometimes hit traffic on the way home. Since we always took two cars, we raced each other up the freeway to the McDonald's near our school. The last ones there had to buy breakfast for the ones waiting. One morning, it got so nuts that we were driving on the freeway shoulder. I was driving, as usual, and was out ahead of Ethan, who was driving behind me. We were both driving pretty fast, coming up on our exit. Suddenly the traffic in front of me just stopped. I had been paying more attention to Ethan in my rear view to the traffic, so I had to literally slam on my brakes; even so, I came within inches of hitting the car in front of me.

One of the guys in the back seat would not wear his seat belt. He preferred to lean into the front and talk over everyone. No matter what anyone said, he would not sit back or stop talking. When I stopped short, he almost went through the windshield. That shut him up.

It felt a little strange; everyone thought this other guy was obnoxious and did not want him around, while here I was, accepted, popular, part of the group. What a turn-around!

Sometime during my first or second year at Windward, my parents began having financial issues. Being a typical teenager, I did not even notice their strain at first. My dad had retired a few years earlier; now he developed prostate cancer. Between taking care of him, fighting her own health issues, and trying to manage the medical center she had built in the Valley back in the mid-to-late eighties—her final project that was supposed to bring in a substantial, steady income for the rest of my parents' lives—my mom was exhausted. She got so drained so often that I became adept at writing out the monthly checks and holding them up so she could sign them. She and Dad kept telling me everything would be fine, I should not worry, but how could I not, when they were both getting stressed, exhausted, and weaker in front of my eyes?

The steroids Mom took to fight her Lupus made her gain a lot of weight, which made her terribly depressed on top of all her other daily battles. I witnessed "true love," the stuff of books and movies, right in my own home. My parents' love for each other never wavered even the slightest. Until the day he died in 2001, my dad was as taken with his wife as he had been when they first met and thought of her as just as beautiful; my mom still wore her wedding ring when she died nine years later. But that year, my freshman year in high school, was especially hard for them. Mom was bedridden or hospitalized more often than she was functional and, consequently, watched from the sidelines as the medical center's potential slid away. Still, she never stopped working. She was an amazing spitfire, consulting from her bed and doing whatever she could, whatever she had to do to maintain the illusion that our standard of living was not changing. Eventually, though, we lost most everything, even the Santa Monica condo we had lived in my entire life. Mom moved us into a beautiful Century City condo that was nicer in many ways and actually closer to my school. Even as my parents declared bankruptcy, she managed to keep the cars and as much of our old lifestyle—at least my old lifestyle—as possible.

I felt I was doing my bit by making as much of my own money as possible. I ran the shows at Lincoln Middle School through my sophomore year and made deliveries for a local pharmacy during the summer. At least I did not have to bother my folks for gas money or cash to go out with my friends.

In fact, I felt pretty independent. I had "caught up" with everyone else and was having more fun than I ever imagined I could have. If Dad had been waiting for me to "outgrow" my early developmental problems, he could have stopped in my junior year of high school. That desire to huddle away alone in some small, dark place that I gave into in seventh grade was supplanted by a sense of new adventure and possibilities. I never stayed home sick; I loved going to school too much-not for the classes, which were okay, but because my social life had sprung to life with a vengeance, as if trying to make up for lost time.

I still ran on the cross-country team, but now I also took on the challenge of editing the school paper. I did everything from coming up with article ideas, to writing pieces, to laying out the pages, to making sure the printed copies got distributed. I had two non-class periods and free reign to do whatever I wanted, so I put together a two-page survey asking people about their sexual attitudes.

"Are you having sex yet?

"How many partners have you had?

"How often do you have sex?

"Do you use protection?

"Are you worried about pregnancy? AIDS? Syphilis or other STDs?"

It was a pretty serious survey and a lot of people responded, with surprising results. Like most teens in those years, I assumed I was the only virgin in my class, maybe even in the whole school. I was wrong; under the cover of anonymous answers, most kids admitted they were not having sex yet. From the vantage point of adulthood, I am relieved that was the case; as the originator of the survey, I secretly felt "part of" again.

I had new sources of income, too. By tutoring an eighth grader in math and chauffeuring underclassmen to and from school in my mom's Jaguar, I earned enough cash to help pay for my own car insurance in addition to my personal expenses. I could not pretend I was only working for money, though; I loved working. My earlier flirtation with the adult world during the Bush election had blossomed into a full-blown love affair with being productive and making things work. I spent most of my junior year feeling high on life. I made eye contact with more people more consistently than ever before. I was not necessarily comfortable with it, but no one knew that but me. I had effectively made all my childhood problems go away, at least in my own mind. Autistic? Never was, never would be. I had friends. I had a decent grade-point average-not as good as most of my friends, true, but certainly better than anyone besides my mom ever expected me to have. I was resourceful. I was responsible. I was popular.

And I was about to get hit with a healthy dose of reality.

At the end of the year, Windward held school-wide elections to fill the following year's student council positions. I decided to run for Student Body Secretary. This situation was more intense than the one in middle school, but the process was essentially the same: put up posters, run a campaign, give a speech. I was a little uneasy about the competition aspect of the election, but I ended up being the only one on the ballot for my position. All I needed was fifty-one percent of the votes, which, with no one else running, should have been a shoo-in. Unfortunately, I forgot about the average teenager's sense of humor, possibly because I did not always share it. Some people thought it would be funny to write in names of kids who were not running or to vote for "none of the above." I actually lost the election—to no one. I did not lose by much, but that hardly mattered. I lost. Against no one. Between me and nobody, the school had chosen nobody. My self-esteem dropped through the floor, while my embarrassment shot to the clouds. All my old issues—Does anyone really like me at all? Am I even likable?—smacked me in the face. I doubt the school administration thought it was all that funny either, but I was the one who had to stand up in front of the whole school again—400 kids plus teachers and staff—and ask them to please give me a chance. It was awkward and uncomfortable, but I did it, and I looked directly into as many people's faces as I could bring myself to as I talked. Three years earlier, I would not have had the nerve. On the next ballot, I won. I wanted it to be unanimous—after all, I was still running against no one—but I had to be satisfied with winning by a substantial margin. Believe me, I was satisfied.

13
Sex and My Senior Year

I began my senior year of high school as Student Body Secretary carrying a 3.3 grade-point average. Almost everyone else in my school, including most of my friends, maintained 4.1 or 4.2 GPAs. They all got 1400 and 1500 scores on their SATs, too. I was no better at taking standardized tests in high school than I had been in elementary school; my SAT score came in around 1000, which I lied about to my friends because it was so embarrassing. Windward was a college-prep high school; we were all expected to attend world-class universities. Toward that end, I had visited a bunch of colleges during a "College Block" my sophomore year. We took a bus up to Davis, the northern—most campus in the University of California system, then toured UC Berkeley, Stanford University, UC Santa Cruz, and UC Santa Barbara over the four-day period.

I applied to roughly ten schools, just as everyone else did, because by then, I was completely out of sync with what I had been through. I dismissed my childhood and earlier academic and social trials. I was just like everyone else. I had no disability. I certainly was not unique, or challenged, or handicapped in any way. Okay, may I had been a little slow in developing, but so what? My problems now were typical of any teenager-any teenager who had to consciously remind himself to look at someone when he talked to them, or who needed extra help whenever confronted with a new environment or situation. I was just like any other teenager whose sole physical prowess was the ability to run and whose life was so pigeon-holed that no one single individual knew the whole of him. I was right in there with all the other teenagers who still did not know to connect the dots between how his thoughts and feelings affected the people around him. Yeah, I was just like everyone else.

Girls were the one thing lacking throughout most of my high school career. I was certainly interested in them; I talked to them and socialized with them as friends. I just could not take it to that next step of asking one out on a date. There had been more girls than boys on that tenth-grade College Block tour, and I had befriended some of them. I really liked one in particular and wanted to ask her out so badly, so very badly, but I could not. I could not do it. I just could not. The teachers did not really chaperone us on the trip, and we had plenty of time to go out together for a burger or something like that, but when we got to Davis that first hot night, I chose to run instead. I ran about six miles. The next day on the bus, the girls were friendly again. I hoped that starting as friends on the tour would help me work up to taking the next step, but those relationships turned out to be temporary. They dissipated as soon as we returned to school. We said hi to each other in the hallway, but it was different. After awhile, it was nothing.

I had no small talk. I was more comfortable darting

my eyes around a person's face than giving them my full gaze. If only a girl had approached me or someone had helped launch me into the activity, like when I learned sailing or stage crew. But that could not happen, because I so compartmentalized everything in my life that I only talked to certain people about certain things and to certain other people about other things. When it came to girls, sex, and that kind of thing, I had no one. I shot the bull with my friends, but did not ask them about girls: none of them was dating yet either. My dad was too old fashioned; I never got that father-son talk that was supposed to clarify everything. I still saw a therapist every week, but we never talked about anything other than my mom and what was going on at home. I kept my social life a tight secret and relegated my sexual emotions and desires to the back recesses of my mind.

I did get up the nerve once to ask Lauren to the junior prom. As a member of the student council I theoretically helped plan the event, but we students had little real say-so about the affair. We wanted a dance in a hotel ballroom or, better yet, a reggae boat. The school decided on a cheesy restaurant.

"This is going to be so lame," I told my date. "Let's do something else." She agreed.

I took her to dinner and to see *Basic Instinct*, probably the worst movie I could have picked. I had no idea what it was about; I just heard a lot of pizzazz about it. Lauren squirmed in her seat all the way through the film; by the end we were both uncomfortable and embarrassed. So much for eye contact: I could barely look at her once the lights came up. I certainly did not try to kiss her goodnight, and I never had the guts to ask her out again.

That was my one major foray into dating for most of my high school career until one day in my senior year, when a girl actually took matters into her own hands. Talk about fulfilling a fantasy!

105

Kadimah was the absolute opposite of me in every way. Here I was, the All-American, blond, blue-eyed, clean-cut conservative boy next door carrying the same name as his father and grandfather. There she was, a tie-dye wearing, pot-smoking, progressive spirit for whom "liberal" was probably too conservative a word and whose name meant "star" in Hebrew. She walked up to me in the hall one day and said, "I've got a problem for student council, but you probably won't take it seriously because you never take anything seriously, and you don't really care about people like me. Do you."

I never expected to be confronted so bluntly out of the blue, especially not by someone so pretty. My mind seized up at the challenge, but my mouth blurted out, "Whatever it is, I promise I'll totally take it seriously."

We both felt an immediate bond that went beyond anything I had ever experienced before. I had made friends before, but Kadimah and I were simpatico on a much deeper level than mere friendship. Not only could we talk about anything, we were both more open and receptive to each other than either of us had ever been with anyone else. Her dare launched a remarkable, life-changing relationship that lasted for years.

Since my first two periods were open that year, we went to McDonald's for breakfast practically every morning just to talk. Over a series of Egg McMuffins, Kadimah told me her life story, which had been pretty terrible up to that point. I told her my life story, minimizing my early development problems—even with Kadimah, I refused to acknowledge I had actually overcome anything all that difficult. I had unconsciously adopted my father's view that plowing through the days the way my mother expected me to had gotten me to where no one thought I would ever go. It might have been fuzzy thinking, but I spent a good deal of time and effort not thinking about it at all, a mind-set at which I was adroit.

Kadimah had doubts about her sexuality at the time,

a matter she did not resolve until long after high school. I probably only added to her confusion by developing serious feelings for her. When she came down with chicken pox, I brought her movies every night from the Pacific Palisades video store where I worked as assistant manager. The store was not far from our former apartment in Santa Monica, but it was quite a distance from her home in the San Fernando Valley and just as far from our condo in Century City. When she talked about her sexuality concerns, I told her how much I liked her. When she persisted in her uncertainty, I persuaded her to go out with me. I loved being with her. I loved dating her. I looked her in the eye often and easily. At some point along the way, we began making love.

As it turned out, Kadimah was not the only new woman in my life that year. I also befriended my tenth-grade history teacher, who now taught my twelfth-grade Soviet Studies class. She was an Armenian grad student at UCLA with some rather revolutionary ideas. We would hang out once or twice a week at Delores', a diner not far from school, to plan our "revolution."

By the end of my senior year, Windward had started changing. A number of students, myself included, felt the school was losing its identity as a liberal, progressive, informal learning environment where everything was welcome. Instead, it was taking on the type of structured environment that, ironically, I had sought when I first started there. Over my four years at Windward, however, I had come to love the school's original nature and appreciate the value of its tie-dyed, long-haired, any-argument-is-valid-if-you-can-support-it ambiance. My fellow students and I wanted the school to embrace its roots, remain independent, and not sacrifice its character just to get more students or donations. We were too young—even our teacher was only in her late twenties—to realize that as entities grow, they change. Nothing stays the same forever.

During our meetings at Dolores', our teacher helped us write a manifesto and plan a sit-in. Actually, it was more of a walk-out: the whole school walked out of class and gathered in the new gym. I led a lot of it, which did not earn me any love or respect from the administration. I doubt we made much of an impression in the final analysis, which is par for the course with most student demonstrations. Windward has the same Headmaster now as when I attended school, and the alumni committee refused to publish my profile after I told the director that my favorite teacher was that Armenian grad student. Apparently she had been forced to leave after we graduated and is still persona non grata on campus.

I suspect the administration knew we had used her car for our senior prank.

Traditionally, every senior class pulled a senior prank, and by that point, I was pretty much my grade's planner. I wanted to do something big, so I called the entire class and told them to gather on campus at 10:00 Sunday night. My Armenian teacher lent me her small hatchback Honda, and I drove it to the front entrance. Another teacher gave us the school keys and security codes. Some people brought wooden planks so we could drive the car up the steps. We were going to put the car in the lobby.

We had to take the doors off their hinges to get the car in—one of our stage crew people took care of that, but several of us had to lift the big glass doors to make sure they did not break. This was all out in the open on a major street in Los Angeles, right in front of the police and our school's security patrols. Miraculously, the police did not come around that evening, and the security patrol, with whom we were all friends anyway, looked the other way.

While a handful of us were getting the car in the lobby, some other folks went a little crazy. They transferred all the stuff from this one teacher's office into the girl's bathroom. A few other people started getting a little destructive, but I shut that down quickly; we were not there to destroy things. We finished with the car around 4:00 in the morning. A lot of people had already left, but I was not going to leave until the doors were back on their hinges, which turned out to be harder than taking them off had been. Some people wanted to just leave them askew, but I insisted that we secure the school. When we finished, the doors were not 100-percent right, but they were on. I did not want anyone to have a glass door fall on them-part of me always thought like an adult—so we left a "Warning! Open Carefully" note on the door. Since it was now Senior Ditch Day, we all met up again at IHOP for breakfast, and then had a pool party in Santa Monica that afternoon at a house only two buildings away from where I used to live.

The school administration was less than pleased with what we did; they said it was the worst senior prank they had ever seen. They questioned our teacher, who was supposed to say we had taken the car without her consent. That just made the whole thing more egregious in their eyes. The students never felt any real repercussions from the prank, but the next year's class was warned that if they tried to pull a senior prank, they would not get to go to Europe, which was another Windward senior-class tradition. I suppose I should feel bad that we ruined things for all the senior classes that came after us, but my adolescent rebellion had kicked in-a bit late, as usual—so I remember the incident with more fondness than shame. It was a lot of fun.

The fact is I had finally gotten to a place in my life where I was just happy. I was comfortable; I was in command of where I was. Home was ever more a nightmare, but I did not go there much anymore. In a complete reversal of my life, school was my happy place.

Even when everyone received their college acceptance and rejection letters, I stayed positive. Most of my friends were going to UCLA or Berkeley or other "world-class" universities. My SATs were not good enough to get me into UC Santa Barbara, up where my maternal grandparents lived, but they were good enough for all the other nine colleges on my list. I chose Pepperdine, a good, solid school in Malibu relatively close to home—and Kadimah. I had some initial feelings of, Gosh, I should've been able to go to... and Why couldn't I get into one of those better schools? But Pepperdine offered me a nice financial-aid package and the kind of flexibility I soon discovered I would need.

Had I not been so preoccupied with Kadimah, I might have been more prepared for the emotional separation of yet another graduation. I might have spent more time in the moments as they came down. I had branched out during my senior year and made a lot of friends outside my little clique; I was probably close to half the kids in my grade. I did not realize how much I cared for all those people until I had to give a farewell speech at commencement; then I broke down and cried. I talked about how much of a blast I had the past two years and told everyone they had been great.

My parents were at the ceremony, of course, as were my uncle and a few other family members. We went to dinner in Beverly Hills afterwards, but I could hardly wait to get through it so I could get to the graduation party to celebrate one of the best days of my life. I was on such a high, I did not realize I had been here before: when I left the Cedar's program, when I left sixth grade, when I graduated from middle school. Here I was, once again saying goodbye from a position of strength and embarking on something completely new—and once again, not taking into consideration how much harder it would be for me to do that than for most other people.

Not grasping the magnitude of what was happening at the time, I just hugged a lot of my classmates and had a great time at the party. Most teenagers probably do not realize how huge a shift leaving high school will make in their lives; I certainly did not. Nor did I appreciate how much my focus had changed during my senior year or how different my path life was about to become from most of my classmates. Truth be told, I was completely mesmerized by my relationship with Kadimah, and everything else seemed significantly less important. That was a truly life-changing summer. I had my great job at the video store, my first credit card, and my first checking account. I had a serious girlfriend, with whom I enjoyed a healthy sex life. I was headed for a prestigious school that would open fantastic new doors for me. I felt very independent. All my previous troubles-the facts of which I now totally rejected-were behind me. It was the best summer of my life, right up to the dinner with my parents that shattered my world into little pieces.

14
Separation Fast and Furious

I left high school as an adult as far as I was concerned.
I still lived at home, but I barely saw my parents; I
worked full time all summer and spent almost all my
free time with Kadimah. Consequently, we did not sit
together until shortly before I started Pepperdine. Over
dinner, they admitted that their financial situation was
not going to get any better, so they could not readily
provide the extra money I was counting on to make ends
meet at college. They were sorry; they really wanted
to help and would figure something out if I absolutely
needed it, but it would be a strain for them.

I was still a good $12,000 to $14,000 short for the
upcoming school year, even with all my school grants
and loans, and the idea of having to cover all that by
myself terrified me. Still, I had spent my entire life pushing myself past my fears. I said, "Don't worry about me
anymore. I'll support myself."

Brave words; I had no idea how to back them up.

I had to attend a three-day orientation at Pepperdine, where I would once again face a new campus, new people, and new circumstances, all of which still scared me out of my mind. Plus, I had to leave my family, because all freshmen were required to live on campus. Even worse, the school's answer to their current housing shortage was to wedge three people into dorm rooms designed for two. The first people I met at orientation, in fact, were my two roommates: Muhammad, a Muslim from Carson, and Ryan, a devout Christian from a small town in northern California. They no doubt found me, a "Beach Boy" Jew, just as interesting as I found them.

As with previous new situations, the anticipation turned out to be more frightening than the reality. Those three days were great fun, almost like summer camp or one of my high-school "blocks." Through get-to-know-each-other exercises, we became comfortable with our roommates and classmates, the campus layout, and the school's academic expectations. In the back of my mind, though, I worried about how I would manage to actually support myself. My $5.50/hour, rigid-schedule job at the video store that had made me feel so great and independent was suddenly a liability. Obviously, I had to leave it and find a real job.

I looked through the job offering notebooks in the school's career office and found an "answering-service supervisor" listing right there in Malibu, just a few miles from the Pepperdine campus. The hours were flexible and pay $7.50/hour, a huge raise. I was hired on the spot—and my life transformation was complete. I was now a full-time college student with a forty-hour a week job, living on my own. Childhood was officially over.

The answering service job was easy. I took calls for celebrities and businesses in Malibu and supervised the other operators. When the phones were not ringing, I could pull out my books and do homework. I typically worked the 3:00 to 11:00 PM shift during the week, plus put in two eight-hour days on Saturday and Sunday. My parents were still in their Century City condo, but I literally had no time to see them—and I admit, I liked it that way. My only day off was Wednesday, which I spent with Kadimah. I went to her place Tuesday night and stayed until it was time to leave for work Wednesday afternoon. Her mother was a Marriage and Family Counselor and very proud that she and Kadimah's dad had sat on the tracks at UC San Diego to stop Governor Reagan's train. She and her current husband took me in even though I was quite Republican at the time. I became part of their family. They had no problem with me spending the night in Kadimah's bed; in fact, they gave me a key so I could come and go anytime. They had three dogs, five cats and made no secret that the husband smoked pot. Compared to that environment, my parents' house, with its ongoing health and financial problems, dragged at my energy and stirred my insecurities and anger. It was best for all of us, the back of mind rationalized, for me to stay away and just take care of the business of launching myself into life. Whenever one of my insecurities tried to crop up, I shoved it down into the deepest abyss of my psyche. I simply did not have time to be fragile anymore.

Knowing that my parents were going to need my mom's Jaguar back—I had been driving it almost exclusively for the past two years—I dropped it off at their place one day, picked up my dad's Mercedes convertible, and drove to Santa Monica to look for a car. The weather was typical for November 2 in Southern California: Santa Ana winds, warm temperatures, beautiful blue skies. Afterwards, I headed back toward Malibu. Billowing black smoke poured up from behind the mountains, but I gave it no thought beyond realizing there was a pretty big fire somewhere. My mind, as always, was completely focused on what I had to do next: get to school, change my clothes, make it to work in time for my 3:00 shift at the answering service.

When I got to the campus, Pepperdine was in chaos. The fire was not at the school, but the air was full of smoke and ash rained down everywhere. People were running for their lives, trying to get someplace they could breathe.

I found my roommates huddled around the TV watching the news. Malibu was being evacuated. In fact, a Los Angeles County Sheriff's helicopter flew over right then, and a sheriff shouted, "Evacuate! Get out! Leave the area!" on a loudspeaker. We all laughed—our entire dorm watched Bevis and Butthead religiously, and the scene reminded us of pyromaniac Bevis yelling "Fire! Fire! Fire!" as he set things aflame.

As the helicopter passed overhead a few more times, people started freaking out. Amazingly, I was not scared. I was eighteen and felt invincible. I even called my mom to let her know I was okay, but she, too, was freaking out. "You've got to get out of there! Come home! Come home!"

How could I go home? I had to be at work a couple miles down Pacific Coast Highway (PCH) at three o'clock. When I called to verify that everything there was okay, my boss actually asked me to come in early. Meanwhile, all my dorm mates were packing everything they could carry into their cars. I left my stuff where it was and went to work, where air was still clear and the sky still blue. No need to panic; we had nothing to worry about. The fire would never come anywhere near us.

Our office was at the end of a driveway off Pacific Coast Highway (PCH), about twenty feet up a little hill. Not long after I got there, someone ran in shouting that we had to leave. "Everybody get out, the fire is coming, the fire is coming!" We went outside and sure enough, our blue sky had been replaced with billowing smoke and falling ash, and the calm streets had been overrun with the same chaos and frantic escape plans I witnessed

116

at Pepperdine. Scott, the owner's son-in-law and the person who ran the place, decided to shut down the office. He wanted to water the roof, so I climbed up on there and hosed down the building while he locked the place up. Before long, flames were coming down the hill behind us, a San Diego Fire Department truck was pulling up in front on PCH and four Sheriff's Deputies with riot gear were running up our little drive yelling, "Get the fuck out of here!"

I never heard a cop cuss before-neither had Scott, apparently—so we decided we better leave the firefighting to the pros. We went down the highway on foot because there was nowhere else to go. People had abandoned their cars because they could not drive them out of the line of fire. It was so smoky, I could barely breathe, so we crossed to the ocean side of PCH, went through someone's backyard to the beach, and stayed there as long as possible. I was afraid I might have to swim away to escape the oncoming smoke and heat, but twenty minutes later, somebody from the fire department gave us the all-clear before rushing off to another hotspot up the highway. I have no idea how they did it, but our answering service and all the buildings around it were spared. I guess the fire just passed us by. The hillside was charred, of course, and gave off a sickly sweet odor that lasted for months. Our power was off, as it was all over town, but we had an emergency generator and were right next to the phone company's central office, so we got back in business within the hour.

Because our phone lines were up and we were "the" answering service for so many businesses and homes in Malibu, we became an information clearinghouse. My mom called and wanted me to come home—unbeknownst to me, my grandmother, her mom, died that day—but I said, "No, I gotta stay here. I'm helping." I was not simply helping; I was making myself invaluable. We stayed on that back-up generator for twenty-hour hours before Edison restored power to the city, and I worked straight through for another eight hours beyond that before I left.

At one point when I needed some air, I took Dad's little convertible to a station a couple miles up the road and brought back a bunch of gas cans for the generator. It did not occur to me that driving cans of gasoline into a fire zone was dangerous any more than it had occurred to me that standing on a roof while fire roared down the hillside toward me was crazy. I was eighteen and invincible! Scott was so thrilled afterward with everything I did that he gave me a raise and a promotion. Out of disaster came personal triumph. Handicapped? Ha!

But while I was riding higher and higher, my parents' life was ebbing lower and lower. My grandmother had taken care of everything for my grandfather. He did not know how to cook, clean, or even take care of the house; plus, he was old and lonely and not in good health. All that, combined with my dad's worsening Parkinson's and my mom's still-minimal earning capacity, made my parents decide to move into Grandpa's Santa Barbara house. They left a few weeks later in December.

That left me finally, truly alone. I no longer had a place to go back to on holiday breaks or over the summer. I was completely on my own, for real—permanently. My parents were gone, my safety net was gone, my home was gone. My answering—service job was now my career.

Somehow, that idea did not bother me. As a Political Science major, I always imagined myself going for a law degree and eventually getting into politics. My mother expected it. Now, though, I realized that as much as I enjoyed political debates and following the news, I had always enjoyed selling things and doing business. Even when I was six, I collected money from my great-grandmother and Nana for a newsletter, The Broadmoor News, which I named after my mom's favorite hotel in

Colorado Springs. Although I seldom wrote anything up, I liked that exchange of product for cash and the idea of offering something to people in exchange for capital. Suddenly, I got excited. What if I shed my high school's expectations that all graduates would become professionals and concentrated instead on being successful in business? With my knack for focus, it was a reasonably easy segue to make. All I had to do was let my academic career essentially fade into the background.

So I did.

15
Climbing My Own Ladder

I was so gung-ho about jumping into business with both feet that I became invested in marketing the company and making it grow. It seemed an ideal situation for me: I was working with all adults, I was helping people, and I was familiar and comfortable in the situation—all criteria that put me at my best.

The owner was pretty happy with the company as it stood, but he allowed me to do some marketing and sales in addition to my other duties. When my ideas began to show promise, I drew up a business plan for expanding things even further, but that did not interest him. "This is great, but you should really focus on school. You don't have to worry about all this."

Wrong answer. Yes, I wanted my bachelor's degree, but school no longer stimulated me. In fact, I never made a single friend at college after meeting my two roommates during orientation. I hung around the dorm somewhat during my freshman year and got my regular good grades, but school simply did not excite me anymore. I had discovered where my true passions lay: business first, girls second. School ran a distant third.

By sophomore year, I was frustrated with my boss's complacency. As far as he was concerned, change equaled risk. He did not care about making more money; he already had a nice little business going, and that was enough for him.

One of our competitors, Howard Goodman, ran a very successful answering service in the San Fernando Valley. He did want to expand and was already doing everything I wanted to do in Malibu. I applied to his company. Howard himself called me to schedule an appointment. I interviewed with him and his vice president, Zan Greenwood, who later became my business partner.

I was nineteen years old and once again confronted with a new situation with new people, but unlike most teenagers who face these kinds of situations, I still battled those old stumbling blocks of my childhood, even though I no longer acknowledged they existed. I still had to consciously force myself to look someone in the eye and still reflexively broadcasted my anxiety: my hands visibly shook during the interview, my persistent nervous cough got worse, and I could not sit still for long without fidgeting or changing position. Zan interviewed me first, reported that I was "completely nervous," and recommended they not hire me. Howard talked to me for a little while before sending me off with a typical "We'll be in touch" dismissal.

Two days later, he offered me a job, but with two conditions: 1) I had to start off at an entry-level position as an untrained operator, and 2) I had to take a pay cut from my current $8.50/hour to $6.50/hour, a pretty big reduction. I decided to make the temporary financial sacrifice because I knew the new company offered room to grow. My Malibu boss had been right: change did mean risk.

My first six months on the new job were eye-opening. Goodman's was much busier than my old place. My ground-level operator's job was both boring and so constant that I could not study between calls. Yet, despite the fact that I hated it, I was surprisingly good at it. I poured all my nervous energy into the work and got to be so fast that I soon became one of the most efficient operators they had. I got a real kick out of having such high statistics, even though my efficiency did not translate into extra money or make the actual work less tedious. But I was the best at something-the best! I could not recall ever being the best at anything before.

My efficiency, work ethic, and tenacity overcame Zan's original objections to me, and by the end of those six months, I had befriended him and his wife Toni, the company's Director of Operations, both of whom were about eleven years older than me. The more I hung out with them, the more Zan became someone I could look up to, like an older brother. In turn, he and Toni came to care for me. They understood how bored and frustrated I was answering phones and knew I felt ready to move up. They helped me work out a plan to take to Howard. My ideas were only a few steps beyond what my Malibu boss had rejected, but instead of shrugging me off Howard said, "Okay. Let's do it."

Just like that, I became the company's first sales representative. Although Howard usually did all the selling himself, he liked my initiative enough to take me under his wing. His marketing plan centered on doing presentations at paging companies. In the 1990s, professionals carried oversized pagers that displayed messages rather than just phone numbers. People called a service to leave their message with a live operator; the operator, in turn, called the pager and typed in the message. Those professionals were Howard's client base—we were that live-operator service—and his expansion plans were all about doing more and more paging-company presentations to attract more and more professional clients. One evening, he said I was going with him the next day to watch him do a presentation, so I should dress accordingly.

I had no suit—I did not even own a coat and tie!—so I made a quick call and drove up to Santa Barbara to borrow a blazer and some ties from my dad. He wanted to teach me how to do up the necktie, but a necktie does not use any of the knots I learned at camp, and I was so nervous, my hands could not master what he showed me. In the end, he tied them all for me so all I had to do was pull them over my head, fit them under my shirt collar, and tighten.

I left Santa Barbara that night and figured I was all set. I showed up to work the next morning in a navy sports coat, gray slacks, and an old-fashioned tie. My boss was not pleased. First he looked me up and down like I was some bum who had just walked in off the street, then he reprimanded me for not being in proper business attire.

I felt horrible, as low as could be—worse than when my mom yelled at me as a little kid—because I was an adult and had gone to such lengths to dress up. Truth was, I had never dressed up like this before in my entire life. Up to that moment, I did not even know the difference between what I was wearing and a suit. Now I was mortified.

That was the end of my innocence, or at least my ignorance. I went out the same day and bought a suit I could not afford-two, actually-and have since never worn anything else for business meetings.

After such a sorry start, I was too nervous to pay close attention to Howard's presentation that day except to realize I enjoyed it and could learn to do it. Once I started selling instead of answering phones, in fact, my job satisfaction exploded. And though I was in a rush to move up, I luckily had to wait several months before my boss decided I was ready to do the presentations alone. By then, I was extremely knowledgeable about both the industry and our company, totally familiar and comfortable with our presentation, and completely psyched about talking to an audience of professionals. Of course, none of that stopped me from feeling scared to death my first time out; I also knew I was nowhere near as good as my boss.

What I had on my side was my youth—I was only twenty-my ambition, and my willingness to learn. I landed a good amount of new business from those presentations, but not because I was such a great speaker/salesperson. I visited the offices more often, which reinforced our already good relationships, and I got a lot of mileage out of being so young. I intrigued people. My little nervous mannerisms and general shyness just endeared me to them. Looking barely over sixteen, I nevertheless held my own in meetings with established professionals in their late twenties and early thirties. People wanted me to be successful and as a result, did more business with my company to help me along.

The more I visited these organizations, the better I became at giving presentations. Before long, people noticed I had a real knack for developing relationships, which is what sales is all about. And they were "perfect" relationships, as far as I was concerned: connection without intimacy. After decades of panicking whenever I confronted new people, I had found the key to easy bonding: it was not about being friends; it was about being friendly. It was about focusing both of us on the mutually beneficial concern that had brought us together while maintaining an affable and accommodating manner. It did not bother me that all my new relationships were impersonal—impersonal was good!

When the company moved to a new, larger facility in Chatsworth that year, my circumstances took a giant leap forward. I had been working out of a cubicle at our old site since I was in the field most of the time. Now I had my own office.

I was in love. I would go there on weekends, stay late at night, even miss class—anything to be in my office. Howard let me work as much as I wanted; I wanted to work as much as I could. I was an executive, a director of sales making $30,000 to $35,000 a year plus commissions. Not too shabby for a twenty-year-old kid in 1995. Of course, I was also a college student taking a full load of classes.

That was the "oops" in my life. I really cannot remember or even fathom how I got through college; the company had my entire focus. I worked sixty hours a week, easy, and was constantly exhausted. I have no idea where I found the time to do anything else. I still managed to bring home Bs and Cs, but it must have been by the skin of my teeth because I missed tons of classes. I just worked, worked, worked all the time. I was obsessed as only someone who used to be content flipping light switches for hours could be.

Howard's company had about 1,000 answering-service accounts, each billing approximately $45 per month. I wanted to reinvent the company as a full-fledged outsourcing call center and bring in accounts that billed $100,000 a month. With his blessing, I wrote letters to big companies and followed up with sales calls to executives on a significantly higher level than the paging-company people. By maintaining my impersonal-yet-sociable attitude, I once again worked my youth to my advantage and managed to impress everyone with whom I talked. That me personally as well as professionally, because I was sensitive about my age, always thinking I was too young.

With Zan and Howard's help, I closed a huge account that doubled the size of the company—and my workload—overnight. The more accounts I closed, the more effort it took to manage them, which meant constantly building and maintaining new relationships. But as I entered my junior year of college, I also had to attend class more often because my upper-division courses were smaller and more intense. It was a hard schedule and a hard life. I typically left my apartment at 6:30 AM to get to Malibu in time for my 8:00 to 10:00 AM class, and then raced through traffic to get to work. When I had an evening class, I got home around 11:00 PM; otherwise, I worked through those hours. At least my weekends were free; I used them to catch up on my sleep!

16
School Slows Down, Life Speeds Up

Two years into our relationship, Kadimah and I had parted ways, which meant my time was truly my own. I chose to focus almost exclusively on work, and my GPA suffered for it. I earned more Cs than Bs and slowed down on my class load so much that I graduated half a year late, in December rather than April, 1997. I even skipped the ceremony to attend business meetings. I learned a lot in college and really appreciated the education, but it just was not stimulating enough to divert me from my work, which continued to be more and more exciting. For once, I was actually ahead of my classmates instead of hurrying to catch up. While they were just now preparing to enter the real, working world, I had already launched myself into the business arena and was halfway up my first ladder of success.

I took all the right courses to get a Political Science degree, so my mom, ever the cheerleading squad of my life, expected me to start law school that spring. No longer interested in becoming an attorney, I instead applied to Pepperdine's MBA Program for Working Professionals and Executives. I could have opted for their traditional graduate school and stayed at the Malibu campus, but I was already an executive, already had the requisite three years' work experience, and was already crunched for time. I had a lot going for me to be accepted.

On the other hand, I also had a lot going against me: a 2.78 college GPA as well as a poor showing on the standardized Miller Analogies Test (MAT), required to get into the master's program. My alma mater accepted me, but their personal letter spelled out why: "You don't have the necessary GPA or test scores, but you just got out of college so we're accepting you on probation. You have to maintain a 3.0 overall and cannot get anything less than a C in any class."

My new classes were in Encino, which was no closer than the Malibu campus but easier to get to with freeway access. I do not know if I was the youngest student ever accepted into the program, but I was definitely the youngest in all my classes; most of my classmates were in their thirties. The first night of class, our professor said, "The vast majority of you will experience a major transformation in your circumstances very soon—definitely before you graduate—simply because you're here. This program is going to change your life."

Talk about prophetic. Less than three weeks later on February 2, 1998, Zan and I left Goodman Communications West and started Greenwood & Hall. It happened almost by accident.

We had been talking about doing something on the side for awhile. I guess as our plans grew, our excitement started showing. When Howard searched our offices the last Saturday in January, we got a call about it from one of the employees loyal to us. We knew the jig was up, so that Sunday we went to see Zan's uncle-in-law, Harry, who had been guiding us through the process of starting our own business. He said, "Even though you guys don't have any investment or anything else, you just have to do it. You have a unified front; go in there and offer to buy your boss out." I don't know where he thought we were going to get the money, but he was a very bold, boisterous, brash entrepreneur and thought we should shoot for the moon.

Zan and I were not that brash, so the next morning we took a slightly softer tack when we confronted our boss. "We heard you were in our offices. Is there anything we can help you with?"

Howard got right to the point. "I know you're trying to start your own business. You're stealing from me." He then asked me to leave his office, which did not surprise me. Zan had been there much longer and had a lot more financial responsibilities than me. Howard probably figured he could live without me—even though I was managing his key accounts and some of them might protest—and use the money he saved to entice Zan to stay. But Zan was ready for that divide-and-conquer tactic. He said, "No, John's not going anywhere. We came in together and we're gonna go out together. We wanna buy you out."

Howard smirked. "Well, someone make me an offer."

The three of us went back and forth for awhile, but in the end, Howard kept his company and Zan and I quit, right then and there. We went to a deli, had breakfast, retreated to my one-bedroom apartment in Woodland Hills and started our company. Neither of us has ever looked back.

I was frightened a lot in my life. Sometimes it feels as if I spent my entire childhood being scared of one thing or another. But this was definitely the scariest thing I ever got into on purpose. I had credit-card debt, I had student-loan debt, I was putting myself through business school. I had no savings whatsoever. Zan made more money than I did, but was in an even worse situation because he and Toni were raising her daughter and had just purchased a new home. The stakes were much higher for him. But we were committed, so we pushed forward. The remarkable aspect for me, which I did not realize at the time, was that it was no longer me against the world—I now had a partner.

We started by going to those clients with whom we had great relationships. Some came with us, and some stayed with Howard. The big one, that huge account I landed that had doubled Howard's business overnight, wanted to come with us, but also wanted to wait and see what would happen with Howard's organization. Ultimately, after playing footsie with both of us for a couple of years, they stayed with Howard.

We worked out of my converted one-bedroom apartment for about three months until we needed more space. Synchronistically, we came across a great opportunity to relocate down in Orange County, where we picked up even more business. The commute was horrible. I drove almost two hours to get to work and another two to make it to my evening classes in Encino. That left little time to actually work, but I preferred sitting in traffic to moving below the "Orange Curtain," as those of us who lived in Los Angeles called Orange County. To me, "The OC" meant three things: Disneyland, the band No Doubt, and Wally George, a local ultra-conservative talk-show host, whose show I occasionally watched for the spectacle of seeing him goad outspoken liberals into fights and then call security to escort them out.

As far as I was concerned, Orange County was nothing more than a business location with no nightlife, culture, or other positive attributes. It brought to mind visits to my grandparents' house in Irvine back in the 1970s and '80s, when the planned community was still relatively new and all the houses had the same sterile look. Traffic be damned: I was not moving down there.

After about six months, though, that horrendous

commute started taking its toll. Pepperdine's Orange County campus was not far from our new offices, so moving would save me money on car expenses and snag another ten hours a week to work. I finally bit the bullet and rented an apartment in South Coast Metro, the most cosmopolitan city I could find. Even so, I could not get used to the place for almost two years. I went back to L.A. every chance I got. Eventually, either the nightlife expanded or I finally looked around enough to notice all that the area had to offer. Either way, I settled in.

Meanwhile, Zan and I worked on growing Greenwood & Hall. What little investor money we had was not enough, so we endured an extremely fretful eleven months, during which both Uncle Harry and my mom continually pressured us to close the company down and find real jobs. That road seemed awfully tempting sometimes, but I had learned tenacity at my mother's knee and Zan was just as stubborn, so we kept going even though it meant slowing down on my MBA schedule for awhile. By the time the calendar turned over to 1999, the business had steadied down. It would take another couple of years and a disaster to really turn things around, but today Greenwood & Hall is a multi-million dollar relation-management company with call centers around the country supporting educational institutions, consumer brands, major non-profit organizations, and government agencies. Boy, am I glad we did not give in to the pressure and stop!

17
The Loves of My Life

I was no longer shy around women. In fact, I had a series of steady girlfriends after Kadimah—one of whom was such a good baker that I put on thirty pounds while I was with her—and had become quite at ease in that arena. I met women at bars, in clubs, and through personal ads in the L.A. Weekly and had relationships with six or seven different ladies every year. Those connections I had been striving for ever since being coaxed out of my private shell now came easily to me.

At the time, I did not realize I only felt comfortable with needy or troubled women who matched my still-struggling self-image. But by 1998, I had a great job, a nice car, and far more confidence than ever before. I joined the new online-dating sites and broadened my focus from one steady girlfriend to dating the field. The more dynamic my life became, the easier I found it to meet attractive women who shared my growing self-esteem and energy—the kind of women I never had the courage to approach or date previously. Like a brimming dam suddenly released, I burst out into the social world and dated every beautiful woman I could find.

I was twenty-three when I met the most attractive woman I had ever been with. She was nineteen and fun and wonderful—but then I met her best friend. I had enough self-control to get my girlfriend's permission before things went too far with the best friend, but not the courage or wherewithal to actually break up with her. I let her end the relationship. My new relationship lasted about a year but was hardly exclusive. Women were everywhere, online and off, and I had as many relationships as I could handle without getting into trouble. I probably slept with ten women in 2000. I carefully never let any of the relationships get too serious. I kept everything light, fun, and feeling good. For the first time in my life, I felt I had something to offer, and I was having a blast being connected with so many women—sexually, not intimately.

Enter Frumi Rachel Barr, Greenwood & Hall's Chief Financial Officer (CFO). Frumi was a smart, nurturing, unconventional, no-nonsense, sexually liberated individual around my mother's age who essentially took over Mom's role in Orange County. One day she handed me a business card. "I know this woman from my gym. She's a little older than you, but I really think you should call her."

No, no. Meeting people online or in a club was easy because everyone was there for the same reason. Calling someone out of the blue to say, "Hi, I'm John, do you wanna go out?" was still too much for the shy boy who lived right below the surface of my public persona. Besides, I was already dating someone else about whom I might one day get serious. She was cute and nice, and I liked her family. We had an easy relationship. When Frumi met her a few months later, though, she shook her head. "Forget that girl. She's not right for you. You've really got to call Julie. Call her now."

I knew my current relationship was not headed anywhere, but I stalled anyway. The woman Frumi wanted me to call was not out looking for dates or part of my normal social scene. She was, in fact, way beyond my comfort zone, the best comfort zone I had ever experienced so far outside of a work environment. Why should I set myself up for such a probable rejection?

Still, Frumi had planted the seed and continued to water it whenever she could. One day—October 20, to be exact—I finished work around 2:00 AM and decided to take the easy way out with this woman: I sent her an email. "Julie, Frumi talks so highly of you. This is me [picture attached]. You sound like a great person. I would love to talk to you." Then I sent off another email: "Frumi, I emailed her, get off my back."

Amazingly, Julie wrote back to say she would love to meet. As soon as we did, I knew she was out of my league. For one thing, she was twenty-eight to my twenty-five; for another, her urbane, upper-class, Chicago-suburban background clashed with my "Beach Boy" childhood. She made $150,000 a year with Alta Vista after leaving Turner Broadcasting; I made about the same, but in my own small, relatively new company that was still fighting to launch into the big leagues. More than all that she was beautiful—so beautiful she radiated. She had a slightly tan complexion, this gorgeous long brown hair, and ... wow. Just wow. No way would a girl like her ever be interested in a guy like me.

Miraculously, she was. She enjoyed our dinner at the Cheesecake Factory; she even agreed to another date. After returning from a two-week business trip, she went out with me again. According to Frumi, Julie really, really liked me. I felt the same, but could not quite convince myself it was real. I spent the two weeks she and her dad went to the Bahamas for Thanksgiving agonizing over my doubts and insecurities. Great—I can't get over this woman. What a once in a lifetime opportunity—if she actually feels the same way about me. But does she? Does she really? She couldn't possibly. Could she?

Recently transplanted from New York, Julie roomed with a friend and her husband in Laguna Beach. Once she returned from the Bahamas, we began spending a good deal of time together, which meant she regularly stayed over at my new place in Irvine. My defenses were still up, though, because I had not been as emotionally intimate with a woman since Kadimah. Then, just before she left to spend Christmas with her family, Julie said, "I'm in love with you."

Wow. "I love you, too."

Her smile was gorgeous. "We're in love; we're amazing. I want to be with you—but I don't want to move in unless we're moving in the direction of marriage." And then she flew off to Chicago.

Marriage. I could not have been less prepared for that kind of move, but I was in love, real love. A month or so later, she moved in, which launched my most profound relationship to that point.

Since Julie was still out of my league, she set about changing my perspectives. Everything I know today about sophistication and elegance I learned from her. My idea of fine dining was The Cheesecake Factory; her tastes ran more along the lines of the best five-star restaurants. Being a gentleman, I paid for everything—to the tune of about $3,000 a month on dining alone! She had exquisite taste, so we went to the Jewelry District to look at engagement rings. The one she liked cost $30,000. Thirty thousand dollars was a lot of money for me—I was still new enough at having money to feel the pinch emotionally as well as financially—but it made her happy, so I bought the ring. We planned to get married at the Hotel del Coronado on October 20, 2001, exactly one year after we first met. The wedding looked to cost about $100,000.

Two days after our engagement party in Chicago, my dad died.

He was eighty-one and had been bedridden with complications from Parkinson's for some time. We all knew he did not have a lot of time left, but it was still a shock. The most devastating part was watching the toll it took on my mom. She blamed herself for his death; she somehow thought she could have kept him alive longer. It was not true, but she was inconsolable.

So was I when I got to the funeral home. I sobbed my heart out for twenty minutes while holding my dad's hand. Julie stayed by my side through the entire memorial service and reception and those horrible hours afterwards, when all I could focus on was taking care of Mom. They say you learn a lot about people during a crisis. Julie learned enough about my relationship with my mother to decide it was too involved. She did not understand it. She did not like it.

Julie already knew about my childhood, of course, but only as much as I told her, and I minimized everything. She had no idea what my mother had sacrificed for me or how Mom had pushed and prodded and nudged me out and beyond the world of assisted living into who and where I was. I could not tell her; I did not know how. It would have meant admitting the truth to myself first, and I was much too deep into my new, wonderful, successful life to even consider going there. Better Julie should just not like Mom that much.

Instead, I started adding up numbers. Business was good, but my pocket was not all that deep. I had put down ten percent when I bought my first house that June; my mortgage was now twice my former rent, my new BMW was a high-maintenance machine, and there seemed no end to the wedding costs. I spent the summer feeling overwhelmed, an old, forgotten emotion whose return I did not appreciate. Julie spent it feeling frustrated, which served to overwhelm me more and push me away from her. Finally, I told her we had to postpone the wedding. The company was not doing so well, my father was dead, one of my mom's brothers, Uncle Greg, had also died, and I could not see my way out of the fuzz in my head. All this pressure would be too much for anyone, I told myself. Frumi and Zan agreed.

That did not help anything, because Julie thought my relationship with Zan was dysfunctional and that I spent too little time with her and on myself. All I thought about, she claimed, was work, which was the one area where she agreed with my mother. Julie wanted me to just say "Screw 'em!" and get myself a high-paying job with security, benefits, and a future. I had naively thought that love meant understanding, but she neither recognized nor cared about the sacrifices Zan and I had made to get this far. She wanted me to walk away from what I had built and go forward with only her. She could make it sound so tempting.

On Saturday, September 8, 2001, Julie, Toni, Zan, and I met at Jerry's Deli to decide on Greenwood & Hall's future. We all knew that financially, the company only had a few weeks to live, if that. Julie pressed hard for us to close and was thoroughly disgruntled when Zan and I decided to keep pushing through. To her, it was a huge risk—but we knew the huge risk we had taken to start the firm. Our guts and souls were invested in this company.

At the time, the American Red Cross was our biggest client. We billed $20,000, maybe $30,000 a month from them if we were lucky. When the twin towers went down in New York three days after our meeting, Greenwood & Hall's fortunes shot up. We did their telethons, we took their emergency calls, we handled all their communications throughout the entire disaster and its aftermath. The million dollars we billed took care of all our obligations with money left over. After that—perhaps because of the way we handled that horrible situation—accounts started coming in. Our business had found its feet, and we were on our way.

Julie, on the other hand, got laid off after the terrorist attack. She had her own money, but now spent her days taking care of the house, going to the gym, shopping, and generally being a housewife. She hated it. And she hated Irvine. Orange County was boring. She was used to Chicago, she was used to New York. She craved the fast pace and sophistication of the big city. She did not care that the company was growing exponentially; she still wanted me to be done with it once and for all so we could move up to Los Angeles, which at least offered some of the trappings of a decent city.

As much as I loved her, I could not turn my back on my partner, on everything I had worked so hard to accomplish, on having the reins of my destiny in my own hands. It took too much to get there, even if I could not consciously acknowledge that reality. Our arguments grew so intense we decided to go for therapy. In our last session on December 31, 2001, we both realized the time had come to stop what had turned into an irreconcilable push-and-pull. We amicably broke up in the therapist's office at 7:00 PM, New Year's Eve. We then went to see a three-hour movie about Muhammad Ali and celebrate New Year's at TGI Friday's. As the evening wore on, I felt a huge burden lift from my shoulders. I honestly thought that since we lived together and still loved each other, everything would settle down and be fine from then on.

I was wrong, of course. Julie was upset, and my naïve reactions only made things worse. She moved out of my house about a month later, but not out of my life. The bond between us remained steadfast, and neither of us could walk away from the intimacy. We even kept sleeping together.

The freedom of living alone sent me right back to

playing the field, this time with even more women. Julie may have raised my expectations, but that did not stop me from wining-and-dining one attractive woman after another, sometimes in the same evening. I cannot recall how many women I slept with in 2002; I only know I went out as often as I could, craving connection (and sex) with as many different women as possible. Online dating services were a boon for me.

I really hit it off with Leilani, a recent divorcee, on Match.com. We met in June, but when I received my MBA, I invited Julie, not Leilani to the graduation. Mom, who now did Frumi's CFO job from her home office in Santa Barbara, came down for the ceremony. Even Shelley and a few of my therapists from Cedars showed up. I had overcome, I had triumphed. I was an undeniable success. Rah me!

As the year marched on, I found my company's steady growth very satisfying, but my non-working existence boring. That November, even though I was supposedly "with" Leilani and was still seeing Julie, I also started sleeping with Jean, another soon-to-be divorcee. Leilani saw the writing on the wall and broke up with me because I did not know how to do it myself. I could not even maintain that dissolution: Jean and I only dated for three or four months before I started seeing Leilani on the side again.

Over the next few years, my relationship with Leilani turned into a song refrain: make up to break up. I still slept with Julie when the occasion arose and saw Jean every once in awhile, but I also played the field without remorse. Leilani knew I loved her; she wanted us to be exclusive even though she also knew my relationship with Julie was absolutely non-negotiable. I could not deal with the idea of exclusivity. That level of commitment outside the business environment confused and frightened me. Even my most intense client relationships were intermittent, confined to business hours, and predictable with interactions that conformed to standard procedures within polite structures and conservative personal expectations. I loved that kind of commitment.

But personal commitments to women? Those remained beyond me. I enjoyed being with women, but to me those relationships were deep friendships with sexual benefits. It never occurred to me that not ending a relationship when I was ready to move on was hurtful. My focus remained too narrow to encompass all that foreign emotion.

When Mom broke her hip in September 2004 and had to spend a few months in the hospital, it only added another level of stress I had to push out of my mind. What if she died? She was terribly depressed; what if she grew so despondent she tried to kill herself? I worried about her constantly, sent her money regularly, and salved my increasing fears emphatically by having sex with many, many women.

Too many women. By early 2005, I was dating five different women. Leilani and I had broken up for good, but I missed her and wanted to get her back somehow. Between working seventy or eighty hours a week and juggling all these women, I went a little crazy, and so did my schedule. That February nineteenth, I made my crowning error: I called off a date with one woman so I could go out with one of the others. The woman I cancelled on drove by my house and saw that my car was not there. She called my cell phone several times. I did not answer. So she rang my doorbell the next morning and found the girl I went out with the night before, who had stayed over.

The awkwardness did not end there. One of the women got into my cell phone, found the numbers of the others, and called everyone.

They all thought we were exclusive.

I had berated myself for weeks at that point: Oh God, how did I get myself into this?! I've gotta clean it up by

March fifth—I can't take five women out on my thirtieth birthday! I have to pick one. But picking one was not the issue; I could not bring myself to disappoint the other four. I knew what it felt like to be left out, and still did not comprehend that these women were not just really good friends with whom I had sex, they were caring, loving people who looked at me as a potential husband. It never entered my mind that my cheating hurt them a thousand times more than simply ending the relationship would have.

All five women were righteously incensed. One threatened to tell the world about my indiscretions; I was afraid it would be all over the eleven o'clock news. I felt like a pariah, like I had broken every sacred law of every religion known to man. What if my clients found out? The women left notes under my door. They came in while I was at work and left pictures of themselves. They sent me letters—they sent me copies of letters they claimed they'd sent to Oprah. Oprah! Good Lord, my life was over. I was scared for my life.

Amazingly, Leilani came to my rescue—not as a lover, but as a friend. I realized I had to get my life in order, so I vowed to not date or have sex with anyone for ninety days. She hung with me all the way through, and that May, I sold my place in Irvine and moved into a new house behind gates.

I did not leave a forwarding address.

Photo by Ana Brandt Photography

18
Am I Still Autistic?

L eilani came with me when I moved. Julie had
moved to Chicago over a year earlier, turning that
relationship into the same kind I still maintain
with Kadimah—good friends—so I managed to remain
exclusive with Leilani for several months, until I met
another girl. Fortunately, we never slept together. Even
more fortunately, Leilani got pregnant, which changed
everything.

Me, a father! I was excited and scared and 100-per-
cent behind the idea having this child. Leilani and I
lived together well; now that she was pregnant, I wanted
to make things work with her once and for all. We got
engaged on Christmas 2005.

Leilani had such a difficult pregnancy that she was
hospitalized for six weeks before she gave birth. We
named our son John Robert Hall IV after my father and
grandfather and agreed to call him J.R., maintaining yet
another family tradition. J.R. came into the world March

16, 2006, fully eight weeks early. He was only three pounds, fourteen ounces. Leilani was not in good shape either, and I felt torn in half. Do I go be with Leilani? Or do I stay with my son? I don't know what's gonna happen to her—I can't let her be alone. But what about him? He's so tiny—I can't let him be alone, either. Who do I go with? How do other people make these kinds of decisions?

I decided to stay with J.R. I held his little hand all day; he clutched my finger. By the end of the day, both mother and child were fine, but while she came home a few days later, he stayed in the Hoag Hospital Neonatal Intensive Care Unit (NICU), an amazing facility, for four weeks. Leilani and I spent as much time with him as we possibly could—I did not want to mimic my own entry into the world, even though I still did not admit I ever had a problem.

Because J.R. came so early after so many pregnancy complications, Leilani and I never had the City Hall ceremony we planned, so we got married in Hawaii that October and then threw a reception back home. All that time, I was faithful; I was a good boy. But when J.R.'s autistic symptoms became noticeable the following summer, I got scared. We started him in therapy immediately, of course, and I did my part to the fullest, but I was flooded with emotions I would not look at and memories I had to stamp down and repress. The fear made me vulnerable enough that when I heard from Jean, we began talking again. A few months after Lia was born on April 29, 2008, we started an affair.

Jean knew about J.R. but not about Lia. I led her on without mentioning that Leilani and I had two children, not one. I kept promising myself I would reveal the truth but never did. I just could not find the words. I had hidden too much of myself for too long, and held myself back from that terrifying level of honest vulnerability. I took care to only see Jean every few months; between

146

the company, my family, and the extra time J.R. needed, I was too busy for more anyway. Still, as sporadic as the affair was, it went on for almost eighteen months. After the first six months or so I started thinking, I'm really not getting anything out of this. Why am I doing it? I wanted it to end, I just did not want to be the one to end it. Look her in the eye and say, "It's over"? I had no idea how to do that. I was back in the same rut that got me into trouble in 2005.

Ironically, I did not want to be the kind of man who cheated. Despite my repeated failure to live up to my own expectations, I wanted to be with just one person in a monogamous relationship. I spent hours trying to figure out what was wrong with me, why I could not surmount this weakness when I had triumphed in so many other aspects of my life. Back in 2005, my mother had insisted that I just had not found the right person yet. As soon as I did, she assured me, I would have no problem with commitment or fidelity. I believed her, but then she never thought any woman was good enough for me and was no more interested in conceding the decades-old hole in my psyche than I was. Leilani, according to Mom, was not "the one" for me, either, despite giving me two beautiful children. "She's a nice girl, but what if she's not right for you? Maybe this other person is right for you." In the last few years of her life, though, Mom not only accepted Leilani, she became very fond of her. In fact, she grew to love and appreciate her.

Connection without intimacy was so much easier. I kept my focus on work as much as possible until the guilt and discomfort of being someone I did not like got the better of me. I broke up with Jean in January 2010. Around the same time, she went to Facebook and learned about Lia. "Do you have a daughter?" she called to demand.

"I do, and I'm sorry. I meant to tell you about that but I'm just... there was never a right time."

That upset her even more, so I decided to make a clean break with everyone in one day and told Leilani about Jean. She took it fairly well considering the circumstances, but we agreed I would start seeing a new therapist, one with whom I could address this issue. She made it clear that our marriage was on the line.

In the course of that treatment, I was diagnosed with adult ADHD. Adult ADHD isn't about focus—I am extraordinarily focused, as only someone who came from autism can be—it is about impulsivity. Serial romantic relationships are a key symptom. Who knew? I had convinced myself I was just a bad person or truly unlucky in love. Leilani helped a lot by going to therapy with me, and the medication I took for ADHD helped a great deal.

Then Mom died.

Ever since she broke her hip three years earlier, I tried to get her to move in with us. We were already an extended family: Leilani's mother lived with us and the kids. I wanted to move us all into a bigger house where everyone could be comfortable and I could look after my mom, but she steadfastly refused to leave Santa Barbara. She had Life Alert; whenever she fell her caretaker got a call, I got a call, and if she was alone at the time, the paramedics got a call. That winter she fell every three days or so, but her mind was still sharp, and she was still a formidable woman; no one would move her out of her home and that was that.

That same January, Mom began acting strangely and slurring her speech. She blamed it on medication changes, but her assistant and caretakers were concerned. When she refused to get the MRI her doctor wanted, I called her to insist on it. That was exactly one week before she died.

"Mom, I'm worried. You need to get checked out. You may have had a stroke. Something is wrong. I'll come up there and drive you myself if that's what it's gonna take! Please do this, for me if not for yourself."

She said no, which naturally led to a big fight. All those years later, we still could not talk to each other without hanging up angry. The next day, she sounded like a new woman, sharper than I heard her in quite awhile. She convinced me everything was fine again. I still wanted her to get checked out, but it felt less urgent. I always called several times a day to check on her, so I figured if anything else happened, I would know.

That Thursday night, February fourth, I phoned while on my way home from dinner with several elementary-school friends I had reconnected with on Facebook. I just wanted say goodnight and tell her I loved her. At eight o'clock the following morning, my cell rang. I will never forget the sound of that conversation with Anita, Mom's caretaker.

"You need to come up here."

"Why, what happened? What's wrong?" Maybe Mom is ready to go for the MRI ...?

"Your mother has passed."

Anita handed the call to the coroner, who happened to be on a ride-along with the fire department that morning. Anita had called 911 when she got to work and found Mom cold and unresponsive in bed. The paramedics all knew her because they were the same ones who came whenever she fell. The coroner assured me no one had broken in; it looked like death from natural causes. He asked a bunch of questions for his report and hung up. I just sat there in bed for another ten minutes. The logical part of me knew this was coming. The logical part of me even admitted she had been miserable and looking forward to death. But the rest of me was in total shock, not knowing what to say or do. The foundation of my world was gone.

We could not go up to Santa Barbara immediately because Greenwood & Hall had to handle a telethon for the Haiti earthquake that evening. I told Zan and some of our employees—they all knew and loved Mom from her years of working for us—but I never mentioned anything to our clients. Leilani and I drove up to Mom's house the next day. It still smelled like her. We went to see her doctor; he said she probably died from a severe stroke. She had already had a few minor ones. We went to the funeral home. Her arm was in the same position as when she slept, so I took some consolation from knowing she probably went peacefully in her sleep.

Leilani and I could only stay in Santa Barbara for about a week before business called, but when we returned home, it was with a handful of Mom's cats. We eventually found homes for three of them, but kept Speedy, her fifteen-year-old diabetic pride and joy, who needed insulin shots twice a day. He was more soothing to me than the other cat we kept and served as a great reminder, almost a bridge, to Mom. He got quite attached and lovey with us, but when he looked me right in the eyes, I felt like he was looking for Mom somewhere inside of me. I knew he missed her; I swear she visited him at night when he cried. We spent a lot of time and money at the vet keeping him alive because she would have wanted us to, but without her, he went downhill pretty quickly. Less than six months after Mom died, we had no choice but to cuddle him while the vet gave him a dignified death. It absolutely broke my heart.

I had made some serious changes to my life before Mom died. I started my doctorate program at University of Southern California (USC) the previous fall, a step that both surprised and excited Mom. A few months earlier, I had put myself on a spiritual course of study, an education that provided a great deal of comfort and support throughout the ordeal of losing her. I am convinced I was drawn to the metaphysical section of Barnes and Noble for just that purpose. Mom and I had such a convoluted relationship that if I had not been spiritually prepared, her death would have hit me twenty times harder. Since I always throw myself wholeheartedly into

150

everything I do, I subsequently worked with Alison Du-bois, the woman on which the show "Medium" is based, as well as other mediums. Knowing that Mom is okay both with how and why she left and that she approves of where I am in life has been a great source of comfort.

Mom's death impelled me to start dealing with a lot of those issues I had stuffed down and ignored, despite a lifetime of therapy. I needed to write this book to get to some of them, yet I know I could never have written it while she was alive. I have a new outlook on life. I am not fearful anymore. I am not afraid of her dying nor of my own death. Much as I miss her, for the second time in my life I feel as if a huge burden has been lifted from my shoulders. I now realize Mom's life was ruled by fear—fear for herself, fear for and about me—and she passed that anxiety on. Over the years, I did a lot of things she was afraid of, but I held back from what I feared. Until she passed, I could not see how most of my non-business choices were driven by apprehension.

Thanks to the increased efficacy of my newly focused therapy, I now understand that my cheating never had anything to do with sexual addiction, entitlement issues, or being a bad guy. I cheated because sex—or more accurately, soft, loving female companionship—was the drug-of-choice I used to relieve my anxiety when life became stressful. Like any other drug, the women could only provide momentary relief; those relationships could never solve the underlying problem. I never became intimate; that would have made me too vulnerable, and I did not "do" vulnerable. No vulnerability, no pain. It was an admittedly tortuous way of going through life, but one I was specifically raised to embrace.

As a child, I internalized the very real fear of my mother dying, and I now learned that this fear had generalized in my psyche to such an extent that it drove everything I did. I could not make tough personal decisions; I could not deliberately hurt anyone or even be honest with myself. I could not look at who I was, what I accomplished, or who I am at all, because anxiety paralyzed that part of my functioning.

I was inculcated as a child with the need to fight through whatever problems I encountered in life. We all knew something was wrong with me, but my mother never used the word autism; neither did I. We all simply agreed that I had to get tougher and fight harder to accomplish more.

As an adult, I always claimed I was "autistic-like." Yes, I lived in my own world, but that did not make me autistic; there was just something wrong with me. And I truly believed I had conquered whatever was wrong with me by the end of tenth grade.

Today, I recognize how much autism took from me and how many issues it left behind that I still battle every day. I now meet people's eyes as a matter of course; maybe someday it will be automatic. I do not sit still very well; I retain that slight nervous cough as well as a general physical restlessness, but thanks to modern medicine, I no longer have Social Anxiety. I now am a social person instead of acting like one. Having shed the better part of my immobilizing fear, I feel rejuvenated and able to do whatever I need to do. In fact, I feel I am in a pretty good place within myself, a place from which I can continue to grow—all of which begs the question:

Am I still autistic?

Dad and I in May 1976.

Enjoying the swings at Santa
Monica Beach in 1977.

One of my therapeutic companions, Ellen, and I.

My dad and I at my grandparents house in Irvine, California in November 1976.

In Dad's USC garb in June 1976.

March 1978.

My 6th birthday at
Cheerful Helpers
Preschool in
March 1981.

At Santa Monica Beach in
August 1977.

Celebrating my 4th Birthday at Cheerful Helpers
Preschool with Dad and Mom in March 1979.

January 1978.

Palisades Park in Santa Monica,
December 1977.

My 5th Birthday at Cheerful Helpers
Preschool in March 1980.

December 1978.

January 1979 on Santa Monica Beach.

December 1977 with my new fire truck
(lower right).

My first little league team –
The Royals in 1983.

1988 at Lincoln Middle School in Santa Monica.

CIF League Cross-Country Meet, Rose
Bowl, Pasadena, California – Fall 1990.

At the ground-breaking of my Mom's building, Wilbur
Medical Center, Tarzana, California in 1986.

Photo by Ana Brandt Photography

J.R. and I in October 2009, Laguna Beach,
California.

J.R. in October 2009.

Photo by Kym Phan Photography

Photo by Ana Brandt Photography

Leilani and J.R,
October 2009

Lia and I, October 2009.

Photo by Ana Brandt Photography

Photo by Kym Phan Photography

J.R. on Valentine's Day, 2011.

Lia playing peek-a-boo on Valentine's Day, 2011.

Photo by Kym Phan Photography

Photo by Ana Brandt Photography

About The Author

John Robert Hall III was born in Santa Monica, California on March 5, 1975. At about 2 years of age, John was diagnosed as severely autistic and slightly mentally retarded. He spent most of his early childhood years in an intensive therapeutic program known as Cheerful Helpers at Cedars-Sinai Medical Center in Los Angeles. Against all odds, by the age of 6, John had shown significant progress and was mainstreamed in a regular first grade classroom with special education support services.

Despite his progress, John struggled through elementary school to catch-up with his peers, make friends, and better relate to the world he was living in. While he persisted and continued to make dramatic progress throughout elementary and junior high school, it was not until his junior year in high school until John felt he was somewhat "normal." John went on to complete high school and embarked into adulthood.

John worked full-time through college and by the age of 20 was a Director of Sales & Marketing for a prominent call center firm. In 1997, John co-founded Greenwood & Hall, a leading customer relationship and student lifecycle management firm. As CEO, John oversees business development, corporate strategy and development, new product development, higher education consulting, and the Company's Enrollment Management Operations. John also manages projects of national interest for Greenwood & Hall. These projects have included the dedication of the National World War II Memorial, the dedication of the Marine Corps. Museum, White House Conference on Aging, the United States Department of Defense Freedom Walk events, the Shelter From The Storm multi-network telethon for victims of Hurricane Katrina, and most recently Hope For Haiti Now, American Idol Give Back, and Stand Up To Cancer.

John volunteers his time as a mentor for college-ready high school students at a urban high school in Los Angeles. He serves on the Board of Directors of Mapping Your Future, a non-profit 501(c)3 organization that improves access to post-secondary education as well as financial literacy. John was also recently appointed to the Board of Trustees of Roosevelt University in Chicago.

John received his B.A. in Political Science and his Masters Degree in Business Administration (M.B.A.) from Pepperdine University. John is currently completing his Doctorate in Education (Ed.D.) from the University of Southern California.

John currently resides in Southern California and has two children, John IV (J.R.), age 5 and Lia, age 3. His son, J.R. was also diagnosed with Autism Spectrum Disorder and neurological disorders.

CPSIA information can be obtained at www.ICGtesting.com
Printed in the USA
BVOW021926260712

296298BV00003BA/2/P